A Reader's Guide to Samuel Beckett

A Reader's Guide to Samuel Beckett

Hugh Kenner

THAMES AND HUDSON

Reprinted 1988

Printed and bound in Yugoslavia

For Robbie some day,
and for his mother meanwhile,
remembering Vert-Galant

others finally who do not know me yet they pass
with heavy tread murmuring to themselves they
have sought refuge in a desert place to be alone
at last and vent their sorrows unheard

if they see me I am a monster of the solitudes
he sees man for the first time and does not flee
before him explorers bring home his skin among
their trophies

How It Is

Contents

Introduction

The reader of Samuel Beckett may want a Guide chiefly to
fortify him against irrelevant habits of attention, in particular
the habit of reading 'for the story'. Beckett does not write
mood-pieces or prose-poems; he has always a story, though
it is often incomplete and never really central to what we are
reading. One radio script, *Embers*, in thirty-six pages of widely-
spaced type, contains a plot interesting and intricate enough
to serve for a longish novel, thought out by the author in the
kind of concrete scenic detail he would need if he were planning
that novel, and yet the story is not really important. What is
important is that we shall experience the wreckage the story
has left, the state of the man who has lived it in being the selfish
man he was. All day he has the sound of the sea in his head,
and he sits talking, talking, to drown out that sound, and
summons up ghostly companions, his drowned father, his
estranged wife, not because he ever enjoyed their company
but because their imagined presence is better than the self-
confrontations solitude brings.

Again and again the Beckett plays and books are like that.
By the time we arrive on the scene, as readers or as spectators,
the story is over, and what is left is a situation amidst which
it is being recalled, not always fully enough for us to reconstruct
it as we can the story of *Embers*. We may make a loose comparison, if it helps, between this aspect of Beckett's procedures
and those of a writer also thought obscure in his time, and the
subject, once, of many Reader's Guides: the Robert Browning
of the dramatic monologues, contrivances from which we can reconstruct past events if we wish, though the poet's interest

was in present psychology. Undeniably Beckett does tend toward the monologue, and has invented ingenious ways to vary it, as when he presents, on stage, an old man communing with words he tape-recorded three decades before, words in which he predicted—thanks to having put behind him the only experiences the old man finds of any appeal—a brilliant future which the old man belies.

Of the many differences between Beckett and Browning, the chief is perhaps that since his protracted time of juvenilia Beckett has never written an obscure sentence. He is the clearest, most limpid, most disciplined joiner of words in the English language today—I cannot speak for the French—and not the least of the pleasures he affords is the constant pleasure of startling expressive adequacy. Even a work whose decorum forbids him sentences and punctuation abounds in lapidary concisions:

some reflections none the less while waiting for things to improve on the fragility of euphoria among the different orders of the animal kingdom beginning with the sponges when suddenly I can't stay a second longer this episode is therefore lost

Try to reconstruct this in memory, and random though its phrasing may look at first you will find your every attempt inferior.

Though vastly read he does not exact great learning. Allusions pass with often sardonic felicity, deepening our pleasure when we recognize them, troubling no surface when we do not. The difficulties, which are not to be underrated, occur between the sentences, or between the speeches. Or they occur when we try to grasp the work whole, and grasp it awry.

Yet each of his works can be grasped as a whole, if we are willing to let the patches of darkness fall where they do, and not worry at them. We shall not find out who Godot is, and shall waste our time trying. Nor are we meant to ask what Godot 'means'. ('If I knew, I would have said so in the play,' said Beckett.) Nothing can be clearer, on the other hand, than what Didi and Gogo, the men on the stage, are doing; they tell us a dozen times; they are waiting for Godot, and we are to leave it at that, and experience *the quality of their waiting*, like everyone else's waiting and like no one's. (In this play, the antithesis of *Embers*, the accessible antecedent 'story' is minimal. It suffices to know there must be one.)

There are many books, many plays in his canon. Beckett has been constantly busy since about 1945 at least, a statement that will occasion less surprise when we reflect that his habit has been to write everything twice, both in French and in English, and to equal standards of excellence; that he is a painstaking writer, who carries a brief text through many drafts, pondering commas and adjectives; and that the number of printed words is no index at all to the amount of thought and human experience and sheer hard writer's labour that may be compressed into a work. We may almost say—it is at least a useful hyperbole—that he has no minor works; each undertaking is of the same magnitude, though some eventually come out very short indeed. Each is a new beginning, with new characters to be meditated on, in a new world. And while some are more successful, more 'important', than others, there is not one that does not throw some light on all the rest. Eliot said of Shakespeare—and to quote him is not to compare Beckett to Shakespeare, since the insight applies to any serious writer—that fully to understand any of him we must read all of him, for all his work is a single complex Work.

But Shakespeare's variety, we intuitively protest — and Beckett's narrow monotony! Not so fast, not so fast; for (again not to press the comparison) Shakespeare contrived to vary certain essentially constant preoccupations—banishment, for instance, usurpation—while Beckett on the contrary has been at pains to unify a surprising variety of material. No protagonists could be less like each other than Hamm (in *Endgame*) and Winnie (in *Happy Days*); no aging women less alike than the chipper Winnie and the elegiac Maddy Rooney (in *All That Fall*). His bums, his down-and-outs, are famous; yet Henry in *Embers*, all three characters in *Play*, and the man in *How It Is* were all of them well-to-do before they underwent the change that has rendered affluence meaningless. Nor is this fact a matter simply of adjectives; it pervades the conception of each character. His situations vary as much as his characters, from crawling through mud to planning how one shall write the account of one's death. Yet similarity strikes us before diversity does. Since the story, to assign one reason, is frequently of secondary importance, he will often use and re-use a story, or a motif, until we are apt to suppose that we are re-reading versions of the same work.

If we read with attention, though, we shall be surprised how very different one work is from another, how completely afresh he addresses himself to each new project. If he holds one thought in abhorrence, it is the thought of really repeating himself. He has never done it.

The torment he has devised for many characters (who deserve it) is the torment of self-repetition, reciting the same tale again and yet again. Clearly the possibility preoccupies him; clearly it is related to his sense that the writer, try as he will, has ultimately only his one life to draw from, and builds each vicarious being on himself. He has given much thought to principles of diversification, and the first, which seems obvious until we think about it, is the one that divides his dramatic from his non-dramatic works.

Though their overlap needs no demonstrating, the plays and the novels are radically different in a way we may forget as we confront printed pages. On a stage there is nothing ambiguous about what we are seeing, while unspoken thoughts are quite hidden; whereas fiction can afford to be most unspecific about what the stage manager must specify, and can dilate as a play cannot on mental nuances. The difference in conception is so radical that while successful novelists have written successful plays (the stage was the fount of Arnold Bennett's riches) probably no one before Beckett has ever excelled in English in both genres: has ever brought not simply marketable competence but creative enrichment to both.

Waiting for Godot—it is historical, undeniable—accomplished what had not been accomplished for many decades, what even T. S. Eliot's impassioned dedication did not accom-

plish: it gave the theatre a new point of beginning. *Molloy*
and *Malone Dies* did the novel analogous service. All three
were written in a single twelvemonth.

'A new start', to be useful, is always, in retrospect, profoundly traditional. Eliot had a sense of how the theatre should
be revived, by the intensification of some popular entertain-
ment, and pondered the music-hall 'turn' as a basis. But Eliot
was unable to finish *Sweeney Agonistes*, and years later chose
for his popular basis the theatre of Noel Coward. It proved
a bad choice. Beckett, following the same principle, chose
right, without even thinking that he might reform the theatre
('I didn't choose to write a play—it just happened like that.').
He proceeded directly from the simplest of twentieth-century
folk entertainments, the circus clown's routine, the silent cinema's
rituals of stylized ingenuity. Laying hold on these, he had a
grasp of a tradition reaching back to *commedia dell' arte* and
with cognates in the Japanese *Noh*, but in a form that expects
no learning in the audience, only a willingness to accept (to
laugh at) the bareness of what is barely offered.

In fiction, similarly, he took hold of the bare irreducible
situation, someone who is writing, and about his own experience,
and someone else who is reading; and as simply as if he had
given the matter no thought he became our time's inheritor
from Flaubert.

This theme deserves amplification. The Flaubertian Revolution was, we know, a matter of style, of the nuanced cadence
and *le mot juste*. It was also a revolution of theme, for after
Madame Bovary the theme of fiction after fiction proved to be
illusion. *Madame Bovary* is about Emma Bovary's notion that
successive men—Charles, Leon, Rodolphe—offer the vast
emotional opportunities to which she feels entitled. She acquired her sense of entitlement from such sources as novels,
so Flaubert's novel is like the novels she has read, from the
marriage and the obligatory adulteries to the theatrical death;
like them, but written as they are not; composed, sentence by
sentence, with a double vision, a simultaneous awareness of her
illusion and of the realities, barely perceived by her, out of

which the illusion is spun. That is why the style is so important; each sentence must walk that tightrope, making Leon simultaneously the not unusual young clerk, in our vision, and the sensitive lover, in hers. Thereafter we encounter a whole fictional tradition of people who live inside stories. Joyce, in *Dubliners*, presents person after person enclosed in some received fiction, the men and women around them virtually transformed into figments. When Gretta Conroy, in the 'The Dead', says of the young man who died, 'I think he died for me', she is placing him inside a story that shall obliterate the commonplace fact that he died of having stood in the rain, and that fiction of hers has more power over her passions than has the living husband from whom she turns away.

The novels of the Flaubertian tradition have tempted playwrights and film-makers, but have never made successful plays or films. *The Great Gatsby* for instance—how shall Jay Gatsby be impersonated by some actor? For he is incarnate illusion, the collective dream of all the other characters. Such a being abides in fiction, where he is created by figures of consummate rhetoric in a medium whose very condition must be that we shall *see* nothing, shall experience only words.

So fiction, since Flaubert created the fiction of solipsism, has turned away from the visible and the palpable: from the stage, from film. And one of the great interests presented by Beckett's career is this, that he tackles for choice just this theme, solipsism, in novels so closed round we can barely see outside them, and still has understood the theme so well he has found ways to tackle it on the stage as well as in novels. Thus *Endgame*, I think his best play, is that apparent impossibility, a play about a solipsist's world, accomplished with no Pirandello flummery. Its world is monstrous, but so is the world we are defining, the world spun about one man who is accustomed to dominate because we *can* dominate our mental worlds. Its grotesque actualities—the parents in ash-cans, the shrivelling of amenities, the nothingness outside the windows—correspond to Hamm's monstrous egocentric vision, Hamm there immobile in the very centre of the stage, a Prince of Players.

Solipsism – view that the self is all that exists and all that can be known.

And if it resembles uncomfortably certain newspaper realities and fantasies of killing and universal devastation, that fact bears also on a quality of imagination that infects the world the newspapers report: a world of street violence, bombs, starving children. As I write this the graves of twenty-five unknown men are being uncovered a day's drive away, all hacked to death for no evident motive, all migrant workers.

Behind work after work of Beckett's we are to sense a loss, somewhere in the past, of the power to love. Krapp, when he made that tape at thirty-nine, wrote in his summary ledger the words, 'Farewell to love'. It is comic now to see Krapp at sixty-nine turn the huge page in the middle of this phrase: 'Farewell to . . . (*he turns the page*) . . . love': the myopic eyes close to the sheet (Beckett specifies myopia, and no glasses), the finger following the lines, the head retracted as the page is turned, the finger seeking the rest of the entry again, hunched shoulders straightening as the head rises to the book's top, the eyes coming to focus, the cracked voice enunciating: 'love'. To such a pass, a notation to be deciphered, has love come, for Krapp. Which is just the point of all that physical exertion between two words. And Beckett is exceedingly careful to spell out the actors' business. Such is the rigorous externality of a play that everything whatever that they do, that we see, is expressive, and will either express the concept of the play, or work against it. So his stage directions are of finical precision, his pauses are noted as carefully as his words, his presence at rehearsals is an invigilation ('He was always there, terribly present and yet silent', recalled Madeleine Renaud who created Winnie), and the general instructions that sometimes appear at the head of the script require careful bearing in mind if we are readers merely. A dialogue between a man and a tape recorder will become empty virtuosity unless the man is played as specified: a clownish aged shell, love long dead.

It is just this order of information, on the other hand, that the Beckett novels have progressively learned to do without. What would be fixed and vivid to a spectator is fluid, hallucinatory, to a denizen, and the novels, from *Molloy* on, have been told from the inside, from the denizen's shifting deliquescent perspective. We may even say that the discovery that freed Beckett to write his major fiction was the discovery, about 1945, of the first person; as simple as that, but no first-person novels before had so fully exploited the uncertainties of some-one remembering, distorting, narrating. Three earlier novels, *Murphy*, *Watt*, and the as yet untranslated *Mercier et Camier*, had employed a third-person viewpoint against the empirical certainties of which we can see the author struggling. In *Murphy* he is elaborately jocular, in *Watt* he is reporting the results of defective research, in *Mercier et Camier* he lets us know that he is content to be arbitrary, the novel, then, explicitly a novelist's fantasy. But by the late 1940s he had made the separation: the first-person vision for fiction, the third-person vision for plays: the inside, the outside; the inside insidious, the outside grotesque. (The radio plays of the late 1950s and early 1960s modify this distinction interestingly. We hear voices, often self-deceiving voices, but by convention we are there to hear them without ourselves being detected. It is not as though anything were being *written*, to entail the self-decep-tion by which one parries with a reader; it is as though we were privy to the goings-on inside an unsuspecting skull. In his stage plays, on the other hand, the players are always by implication aware of the audience.)

A universe where love has been frozen, then, an insidiously plausible universe, a universe that bubbles up into visible grotesques; and a universe that its creator did not happen upon until relatively late in life, after he was forty. It is most unusual for a major writer to find his direction so late. One explanation, helpful so far as it goes, is that the war made the difference: specifically, the experience of living in France during the Occupation's systematized cruelties. I shall be developing this theme later in the book, while hoping the reader will not make too much of it. Major talent is not so easily explained, and considering the millions of lives on which the war touched, it is surprising how little artistic expression can be attributed to it.

No, Beckett was groping from very early in life toward the direction the experience of the war confirmed, supplying him as it did so with pertinent major metaphors. He prepared himself for an academic career and then threw it up. After his father died (1933) he commenced a life of uprootedness; lived in London for a while, wandered in Europe without apparent aim (how many of his fictional beings are wanderers!), settled in Paris in 1936, all the time writing stories, poems, a single novel (*Murphy*). The whole career up to the beginning of the Occupation looks like a directionless looking for a direction, in confidence only that the available directions—a professor's, for instance, or James Joyce's—were right for other people but not for him.

The man who found his direction in the mid-1940s is now, in Paris in the early 1970s, unfailingly courteous with others looking for theirs. Courtesy, generosity, it has often been noted, are the primary qualities of the man. Let me endorse such remarks without amplifying on them. I have not troubled Mr Beckett about this project, and have not quoted any conversations except for remarks, made to others or to me, that have appeared in print before.

A final word about what this book proposes. First, it sets itself bibliographical limits. It discusses nothing of which the mature Beckett has not sanctioned the publication in volume form. In *Samuel Beckett: His Works and His Critics*, compiled by Raymond Federman and John Fletcher the student will find copious listings from periodicals of the 1930s; I am as willing as Mr Beckett that pieces still uncollected shall remain so.

Second, though the literature about Beckett is now of huge extent, I have mentioned none of it whatever, beyond quoting from Alec Reid's little book on the plays two sentences I admired, and excerpting from Lawrence Harvey's *Samuel Beckett, Poet and Critic* (Princeton, 1970) a bit of an unpublished novel I have not read. (I am also indebted to Professor Harvey's work for many facts about Beckett's early life.) My purpose has not been to slight any critic, but to preserve a singleness of aim.

What I say in the pages that follow I derive, almost naively, from Beckett's actual text, hoping to help the reader see what it is he is reading with as little distraction as possible. In another book, *Samuel Beckett*, I treated the subject quite differently, following themes from work to work and seeking to emphasize its coherence and unity. In the present book the stress falls on the uniqueness of each work, and the impression I hope to leave is one of surprising variety. I am glad to have had the chance to cover a second time ground about which meanwhile I have not changed my mind in any important particular.

Reader's Guides are normally chronological. This one is not, because Beckett was a long time finding his way, and beginning at the beginning is a mistake. To make anything at all of his earlier work one needs to sense the quality of his mature imaginings. Fortunately, there is a sanctioned place to begin. Nearly everyone first encounters Beckett through *Waiting for Godot*, so my commentary does the same. I then double back to the poems and early stories, and proceed from them more or less chronologically, permitting general reflections to arise as they will and trusting that their pertinence elsewhere will be obvious though I have seldom reinforced it. Apart from this strategic displacement of *Waiting for Godot*, my chief violations of chronological order have been the annexing of comments on the late poems to discussion of the early ones, the segregation into a single chapter of all the works for radio, film and television, and the placing of *How It Is* after the last stage plays instead of before them.

Only the English versions are discussed, whether they were written first or second. The alert reader will notice, for instance, one or two references to *How It Is* (1964) as a work of 1959, though that is the year in which its French original, *Comment c'est*, was written. On such occasions I am dating Beckett's conception, not the execution I discuss. I have included a few remarks on *Mercier et Camier* because it elucidates one or two aspects of the existing English canon, and an English version now in preparation will join the canon eventually. Mr Beckett has kindly supplied interim drafts of this version for my quotations from this novel.

Chronology of the Works

This is simply a skeleton listing, to indicate (1) when Beckett was occupied with a project, and (2) when it became available to the reading public. No effort has been made to list magazine excerpts, nor the variously titled collections in which short pieces have been reissued. For full details see Federman and Fletcher, *Samuel Beckett: His Work and His Critics* (1970).

	DATE OF WRITING	DATE OF PUBLICATION
1929	*Whoroscope* (poem)	
1930	*Proust*	*Whoroscope*
1931		*Proust*
1932	*A Dream of Fair to Middling Women* (novel: unpublished)	
1933	*More Pricks Than Kicks* (stories)	
1934		*More Pricks Than Kicks*
1935	*Murphy* (novel)	*Echo's Bones* (poems, written 1931-5)
1938		*Murphy*
1939	French translation of *Murphy*	
1942–4	*Watt* (novel)	
1945	*Mercier et Camier* (novel—French)	
1945–6	*Nouvelles* ('La Fin', 'L'Expulse', 'Le Calmant', 'Premier Amour')	
1947	*Eleutheria* (play in French: unpublished)	*Murphy* (French version)

1947–9	*Molloy* (novel in French)	
	Malone Meurt (novel in French)	
	En Attendant Godot (play)	
1949–50	*L'Innommable* (novel)	
	Mexican Poetry (commissioned translations)	
1950	*Textes Pour Rien*	
1951		*Molloy* (French)
		Malone Meurt
1952		*En Attendant Godot*
1953	English version of *Molloy*	*Watt* (English)
		L'Innommable
1954	*From an Abandoned Work*	*Waiting for Godot*
1955		*Nouvelles et Textes pour rien*
		Molloy (English version)
1956	English version of *Malone Meurt*	*Malone Dies*
	Fin de Partie (play)	*From an Abandoned Work*
	All That Fall (radio play)	
1957	English version of *Fin de Partie*	*Fin de Partie*
	English version of *L'Innommable*	*All That Fall*
		Tous ceux qui tombent (French version of *All That Fall*)
1958	*Krapp's Last Tape* (play)	*Krapp's Last Tape*
		Endgame
		The Unnamable
		Mexican Poetry

1959	*Embers* (radio play)	*Embers*
	Comment c'est (novel)	*La Dernière Bande* (French version of *Krapp's Last Tape*)
		Cendres (French version of *Embers*)
1961	*Happy Days* (play)	*Happy Days*
		Poems in English
		Comment c'est
1962	*Words and Music* (radio play)	*Words and Music*
1963	*Play*	*Oh les beaux jours* (French version of *Happy Days*)
	How It Is (English version of *Comment c'est*)	*Cascando* (radio play: French and English versions)
	Film	
1964	Production of *Film*, starring Buster Keaton	*Play*
		Comédie (French version of *Play*)
		How It Is
1965	*Come and Go* (tiny play)	*Imagination morte imaginez*
		Imagination Dead Imagine
1966	*Eh Joe* (television play)	*Dis Joe* (French version of *Eh Joe*)
		Va et vient (French version of *Come and Go*)
		Paroles et musique (French version of *Words and Music*)
		Assez
		Bing
1966–70	*Le Dépeupleur*	

1967	*Eh Joe*
	Film
	Come and Go
	D'un ouvrage abandonné (French version of *From an Abandoned Work*)
	Poémes (collected French poems)
	Stories and Texts for Nothing (English version of *Nouvelles et Textes pour rien*)
	Enough (English version of *Assez*)
	Ping (English version of *Bing*)
1968	*Watt* (French version)
	L'Issue
1969	*Sans*
1970	*Mercier et Camier*
	Premier Amour
	Lessness (English version of *Sans*)
	Le Dépeupleur
1971 (?)	*The Lost Ones* (English version of *Le Dépeupleur*)

1 Waiting for Godot

Robinson Crusoe, a romance about one man rebuilding the world, becomes a different kind of book when his island proves to contain a second man, black Friday. A *pair* of men has an irreducibly primitive appeal. They can talk to one another, and it soon becomes clear how little either one is capable of saying. Each is 'a little world made cunningly', each has enjoyed many many thousands of hours of the fullest consciousness of which he is capable, each has learned to speak, and learned to cipher, and seen perhaps many cities like Odysseus, or perhaps just Manchester. Each has been torn by passions, each has known calm, each has ingested a universe through his five senses, and arranged its elements in his mind for ready access according to social and pedagogical custom. And they can share almost none of all this. Toward one another they turn faces that might almost as well be blank spheres, and wonderful as words are they can speak, each of them, but one word at a time, so that they must arrange these words in strings, poor starved arrangements, virtually empty by comparison with all that presses within them to be said.

On the first page of his last novel, *Bouvard et Pécuchet*, Flaubert in his fierce drive after essentials described an empty street like an empty stage; caused two men to enter this place from opposite sides and sit down simultaneously on the same bench; saw to it that the day should be so hot they would remove their hats to wipe their brows; and had each, naturally, set his hat down on the bench.

. . . And the smaller man saw written in his neighbour's hat, 'Bouvard', while the latter easily made out in the cap of the individual wearing the frock-coat the word 'Pécuchet'.

'Fancy that', he said. 'We've both had the idea of writing our names in our hats.'

'Good heavens, yes; mine might be taken at the office.'

'The same with me; I work in an office too.'

So begins the mutual disclosure of two mortals, two immortal souls; and what they have to disclose, though lifetimes would not suffice, is somehow packed into the hemispherical spaces those hats were made to enclose.

Beckett's immediate model for the pair of men in *Waiting for Godot* would seem to be less literary than this. Didi and Gogo in their bowler hats, one of them marvellously incompetent, the other an ineffective man of the world devoted (some of the time) to his friend's care, resemble nothing so much as they do the classic couple of 1930s cinema, Stan Laurel and Oliver Hardy, whose troubles with such things as hats and boots were notorious, and whose dialogue was spoken very slowly on the assumption that the human understanding could not be relied on to work at lightning speed. The *mise-en-scène* of their films was a country of dreams, at least in this respect, that no explanation of their relationship was ever ventured. They journeyed, they undertook quests, they had adventures; their friendship, tested by bouts of exasperation, was never really vulnerable; they seemed not to become older, nor wiser; and in perpetual nervous agitation, Laurel's nerves occasionally protesting like a baby's, Hardy soliciting a philosophic calm he could never quite find leisure to settle into, they coped. Neither was especially competent, but Hardy made a big man's show of competence. Laurel was defeated by the most trifling requirements. Hence, in *Way Out West* (1937):

HARDY: Get on the mule.
LAUREL: What?
HARDY: Get *on* the mule.

which comes as close as we need ask to the exchange in the
last moments of *Godot*:

VLADIMIR: Pull on your trousers.
ESTRAGON: What?
VLADIMIR: Pull on your trousers.
ESTRAGON: You want me to pull off my trousers?
VLADIMIR: Pull ON your trousers.
ESTRAGON   (*realizing his trousers are down*): True.
              He pulls up his trousers.

In the same film there is much fuss with Laurel's boots, the
holes in which he patches with inedible meat, thus attracting
unwanted dogs. *Waiting for Godot* begins:

> *Estragon, sitting on a low mound, is trying to take off his boot.*
> *He pulls at it with both hands, panting. He gives up, exhausted,*
> *rests, tries again. As before. Enter Vladimir.*
> ESTRAGON   (*giving up again*): Nothing to be done.

Insofar as the play has a 'message', that is more or less what
it is: 'Nothing to be done.' There is no dilly-dallying; it is
delivered in the first moments, with the first spoken words, as
though to get the didactic part out of the way. And yet they
go on *doing*, if we are to call it doing. There is a ritual exchange
of amenities, from which we learn that Vladimir (as it were,
Hardy) takes pride in his superior savoir-faire ('When I think
of it . . . all those years . . . but for me . . . where would you
be . . . (*Decisively.*) You'd be nothing more than a little heap
of bones at the present minute, no doubt about it'). We also
learn that if Estragon has chronic foot trouble, Vladimir has
chronic bladder trouble. The dialogue comes round again to
the theme words, 'Nothing to be done', this time spoken by
Vladimir; and as he speaks these words the action also comes
round to where it started, with Estragon by a supreme effort
belying the words and pulling off his boot. That is one thing
accomplished anyhow.

He peers inside it, feels about inside it, turns it upside down, shakes it, looks on the ground to see if anything has fallen out, finds nothing, feels inside it again, staring sightlessly before him.

These are instructions to an actor, though few actors succeed in finding out how to follow them. It is just here that many productions begin to go astray, the actor supposing that he is called upon to enact something cosmic. Either that, or he patters through the gestures mindlessly, in a hurry to get to something he can make sense of. His best recourse would be to imagine how Stan Laurel would inspect the interior of a boot, intent as though an elephant might drop out of it, or some other key to life's problems.

We have here a problem of style, to be confronted before we proceed. There is something misleading about this printed text, and yet the perusal of the printed text is one of the only two ways of encountering *Waiting for Godot*, the other being at a performance that may have gone totally wrong because of the way the actors and the director responded to the printed text. And yet the printed text is the score for a performance, and is not meant in any final way for reading matter. Therefore we had better be *imagining* a performance at least. This means imagining men speaking the words, instead of ourselves simply reading over the words. The words are not statements the author makes to us, the words are exchanged. 'Nothing to be done' is apt to sit on the printed page like the dictum of an oracle. 'Nothing to be done,' addressed by Estragon ('*giving up again*') to the problem of removing his boot, is a different matter. It expresses his sense of helplessness with respect to a specific task. There may be, in other contexts, something to be done, though he is not at the moment prepared to envisage them.

But we are in a play, and not in the great world that abounds in 'other contexts', and must wait for such contexts as the play chooses to afford in its own good time. Much as Laurel and Hardy must be understood to exist only within that strange universe the Laurel and Hardy film, so the actors exist inside the universe of this play. If that universe should prove to contain only two themes, the need to take off a boot and the impossibility of doing it, the nature of dramatic universes would not be contradicted. Esteemed plays have been built out of elements scarcely more numerous, for instance the obligation to keep Agamemnon from being killed, and the impossibility of this.

The actors exist inside the universe of the play. But—here is a further nuance—they are live actors, living people whose feet resound on floorboards, whose chests move as they breathe, and we must learn to understand, with a corner of our attention, that they are *imprisoned* inside this play. They are people with opinions and digestions, but their freedom tonight is restricted. They are not at liberty to speak any words but the words set down for them, which are not inspiriting words. (In another Beckett play one actor's question, 'What is there to keep me here?' is unanswerably answered by the other actor: 'The dialogue.') This is always true in plays, as generally in films: it is by following a script that the actors give us the illusion that they are free, and if an actor forgets his lines we discern from his stricken face how little free he is to improvise.

So it is up to the actor to take very seriously the world of the play, which is the only world (and the only play) he is understood to know; and if in the world of the play he is instructed to examine the interior of his boot, why, let him not think of 'meaning' but let him examine it. There is nothing else to be done.

'Sam,' asked an actor at a rehearsal of *Endgame*, 'How do I say to Hamm, "If I knew the combination of the safe, I'd kill you."?' And Sam Beckett answered quietly, 'Just think that if you knew the combination of the safe, you would kill him.'

This play's world contains more than Vladimir and Estragon. Before the pair have been on stage three minutes, we learn of the existence of some folk called 'they', who administer beatings. Estragon says he spent the night in a ditch, 'over there', and on being asked if they didn't beat him, responds that certainly they beat him. The same lot as usual? He doesn't know. 'They' and their beatings need no explanation; as much as the sunrise, they are part of this world. The Eiffel Tower, though not hereabouts, is also part of this world, with custodians so fastidious they wouldn't let our pair enter the elevator. Things were not always so. The two before us were once themselves fastidious. Back in those days ('a million years ago, in the nineties') they might have had the sense to lose' heart, and gone 'hand in hand from the top of the Eiffel Tower, among the first'. It is too late now.

What else is part of this world? Memories of the Bible, a proper Protestant Bible with coloured maps at the back. The need to fill up time with conversation ('Come on, Gogo, return the ball, can't you, once in a way?'). Utter impoverishment of local amenities (the only thing to look at is not much of a tree, so nondescript it is perhaps a shrub). And an obligation:

> Let's go.
> We can't.
> Why not?
> We're waiting for Godot.
> (*despairingly*) Ah!

He is said to have said we were to wait by the tree, if this is the tree he meant, and if this is the day.

> He didn't say for sure he'd come.
> And if he doesn't come?
> We'll come back tomorrow.
> And then the day after tomorrow.
> Possibly.
> And so on.

'Godot', let it be stipulated, is pronounced Go-*dough*, accent on the second syllable. The play moreover was written and for some time performed only in French, so it seems largely an accident of the English language that has caused so many readers (some of whom say '*God*-oh') to be distracted by the bit of dialogue that speaks of 'a kind of prayer' and 'a vague supplication' some moments after mention of Godot. It is simpler by far to stay inside the play, and dismiss interpretations. Godot, inside the play, is the mysterious one for whom we wait. It is not clear why we wait, except that we said we would, and there are hints that he has it in his power to make a difference. 'Let's wait till we know exactly how we stand.'

Once upon a time, it is worth recalling, there was an audience for this play not a man of whom knew that Godot would never come. It would be nearly impossible to recruit such an audience now, or even such a reader, much as it would be impossible to find a reader for whom there really exists the open possibility that Hamlet will take revenge and then marry Ophelia. Everyone knows that this is the Play about Waiting for the Man who Doesn't Come, and it is curious how little difference this knowledge makes. If, to the hypothetical innocent viewer, Godot's coming is an open possibility, still he is not encouraged to expect Godot, or to expect anything of him. The play constructs about its two actors the conditions and the quality of waiting, so much so that no one blames the dramatist's perverse whim for the withholding of Godot and the disappointment of their expectations.

Someone however does come: Pozzo comes. He makes so theatrical an entrance that Estragon easily supposes he is Godot. Of course Estragon is impressionable, but apparently Vladimir supposes it as well, though he quickly denies that any such thought crossed his mind ('You took me for Godot'. 'Oh no, Sir, not for an instant, Sir'.) From this exchange, and from Pozzo's stern interrogation ('Who is he?' and 'Waiting? So you were waiting for him?') and from their hasty disavowals ('We hardly know him' and 'Personally I wouldn't know him even if I saw him') we gather that the world of the play is one in which it is prudent to know as little as possible. And Pozzo, for all his habit of command, appears to be in flight across the blasted landscape, his servant loaded with what may be loot but is more likely salvage: a heavy bag, a folding stool, a picnic basket, a greatcoat. The rope that joins them, the whip with which Pozzo threatens, are symbols of authority, indispensible because custom, the normal bond of authority, seems to have broken down.

Very well. Two men waiting, for another whom they know only by an implausible name which may not be his real name. A ravaged and blasted landscape. A world that was ampler and more open once, but is permeated with pointlessness now. Mysterious dispensers of beatings. A man of property and his servant, in flight. And the anxiety of the two who wait, their anxiety to be as inconspicuous as possible in a strange environment ('We're not from these parts, Sir') where their mere presence is likely to cause remark. It is curious how readers and audiences do not think to observe the most obvious thing about the world of this play, that it resembles France occupied by the Germans, in which its author spent the war years. How much waiting must have gone on in that bleak world; how many times must Resistance operatives—displaced persons when everyone was displaced, anonymous ordinary people for whom every day renewed the dispersal of meaning—have kept appointments not knowing whom they were to meet, with men who did not show up and may have had good reasons for not showing up, or bad, or may even have been taken; how often must life itself not have turned on the skill with which over-conspicuous strangers did nothing as inconspicuously as possible, awaiting a rendezvous, put off by perhaps unreliable messengers, and making do with quotidian ignorance in the principal working convention of the Resistance, which was to let no one know any more than he had to.

We can easily see why a Pozzo would be unnerving. His every gesture is Prussian. He may be a Gestapo official clumsily disguised.

Here is perhaps the playwright's most remarkable feat. There existed, throughout a whole country for five years, a literal situation that corresponded point by point with the situation in this play, and was so far from special that millions of lives were saturated in its desperate reagents, and no spectator ever thinks of it. Instead the play is ascribed to one man's gloomy view of life, which is like crediting him with having invented a good deal of modern history. Not that modern history, nor the Occupation, is the 'key' to the play, its solution;

it is simply, if we do happen to think of it, a validation of the play. And Beckett saw the need of keeping thoughts of the Occupation from being too accessible, because of the necessity to keep the play from being 'about' an event that time has long since absorbed. Sean O'Casey's plays, being 'about' the Irish troubles, slide rapidly into the past, period pieces like the photographs in old magazines. *Waiting for Godot* in the 1970s is little changed from what it was the day it was first performed in 1953, a play about a mysterious world where two men wait. We may state its universality in this way: only a fraction of the human race experienced the German occupation of France, and only a fraction of that fraction waited, on Resistance business, for some Godot. But everyone, everywhere, has waited, and wondered why he waited.

There were plays, once, about the House of Atreus, which touched on the racial genealogy of the spectators, and on the origins of customs vivid to them daily. Such plays hold interest today only thanks to the work of time, which has greatly modi-fied them. What seemed fact once seems made up now, part of the set of conventions we must learn and absorb, and the dramatic doings—Agamemnon's murder, Cassandra's rant—have acquired the authority of powerful abstractions. The effort of Beckett's play in suppressing specific reference, in denying itself for example the easy recourse of alarming audiences with references to the Gestapo, would seem to be like an effort to arrive directly at the result of time's work: to perform, while the play is still in its pristine script, the act of abstrac-tion which change and human forgetfulness normally perform, and so to arouse not indignation and horror but more settled emotions. We seem to be a long way from Laurel and Hardy, but the formula of the play was to move the world of the Oc-cupation into Laurel and Hardy's theatre, where it becomes something rich and strange, as do they.

So the play is not 'about'; it is itself; it is a play. This sounds impossibly arty unless we reflect that *Hamlet*, for instance, is not about dynastic irregularities in Denmark, a subject in which no Dane could now beat up an interest, but about Hamlet, who exists only thanks to fortunate collusion between one man who wrote a script and other men who act it out, and still others who read it. No one at the theatre finds this fact esoteric. It is only students of printed texts who are apt to worry about Hamlet's age, or speculate about his experiences at the University (i.e., offstage). The student of printed texts is apt to conjure up all manner of potential difficulties which in practice, in the theatre, trouble no one. Literary people in the eighteenth century supposed that the famous 'unities' corresponded to inviolable laws, trespasses against which could reduce a play to mish-mash; it remained for Dr Johnson to assert what every frequenter of the playhouse found so self-evident he gave no thought to it, that an audience which can imagine itself in Rome will have no difficulty imagining five minutes later that it is in Alexandria, or for that matter that a jealous man in a play may quite plausibly be inflamed by rudimentary tomfoolery with a handkerchief. We can put this more abstractly, and say that *Antony and Cleopatra* and *Othello* present, when acted, self-sufficient worlds containing their own order of reality, which need not 'mean'.

So. They are waiting. And they will wait for the duration of the second act as well. We have all waited, perhaps not by a tree at evening or on a country road, but waited. The details are immaterial.

They are waiting 'for Godot'. Each of us has had his Godot, if only someone from whom, for several days, we have expected a letter.

The substance of the play, in short, is as common a human experience as you can find. This seems hardly worth saying, except that it is so seldom said. To read critics, or to listen to discussion, we might well suppose that the substance of the play was some elusive idea or other, and not a very well expressed idea since there is so much disagreement about what it is.

The substance of the play is waiting, amid uncertainty. If there has never been a play about waiting before, that is because no dramatist before Beckett ever thought of attempting such a thing. It seems contrary to the grain of the theatre, where the normal unit is the event, and where intervals between events are cleverly filled so as to persuade us that the cables are weaving and tightening that shall produce the next event. Throughout much of the *Agamemnon* the audience is waiting, waiting for Agamemnon to be killed. The Chorus too is waiting till a doom shall fall, and Cassandra also is waiting for this to happen, and meanwhile is filling the air with predictions no one will listen to (and she knows that they will not listen; she is under a curse of that order). And Clytemnestra is waiting until it shall be time to kill him. But this is different. Aeschylus' play as it draws toward its climax tugs its climax into the domain of the actual. To wait for the inevitable is a waiting of a different quality, so much so that were Agamemnon not killed the play would seem a fraud. But it is no fraud that Godot does not come.

To wait; and to make the audience share the waiting; and to explicate the quality of the waiting: this is not to be done with 'plot', which converges on an event the non-production of which will defraud us, nor yet is it to be done by simply filling up stage time: by reading the telephone book aloud for instance. Beckett fills the time with beautifully symmetrical structures.

In the meantime let us try and converse calmly, since we are incapable
   of keeping silent.
You're right, we're inexhaustible.
It's so we won't think.
We have that excuse.
It's so we won't hear.
We have our reasons.
All the dead vocies.
They make a noise like wings.
Like leaves.
Like sand.
Like leaves.
   Silence.
They all speak at once.
Each to itself.
   Silence.

Rather they whisper.
They rustle.
They murmur.
They rustle.
  Silence.
What do they say?
They talk about their lives.
To have lived is not enough for them.
They have to talk about it.
To be dead is not enough for them.
It is not sufficient.
  Silence.
They make a noise like feathers.
Like leaves.
Like ashes.
Like leaves.
  Long silence.
Say something!
I'm trying.
  Long silence.
(*in anguish*). Say anything at all!
What do we do now?
Wait for Godot.
Ah!
  Silence.
This is awful!

In a beautiful economy of phrasing, like cello music, the voices
ask and answer, evoking those strange dead voices that speak,
it may be, only in the waiting mind, and the spaced and measured
silences are as much a part of the dialogue as the words. And
the special qualities of the speakers are never ignored. Estragon
insists that these voices rustle, and like leaves; Vladimir, less
enslaved by idiom, will have it that they murmur, and like wings,
or sand, or feathers, or ashes; but Estragon's simple trope is,
thanks to his sheer stubbornness, in each case the last word.
And the utterances are gradually reduced from sixteen words
to two, and the ritual exchange about waiting for Godot has
its ritual termination like an Amen, the shortest utterance in

the play, the monosyllable 'Ah!'. It is a splendid duet, to make the hearts of worthy actors sing, and contrary to theatrical custom neither part dominates.

As the speeches are symmetrically assigned, so the two acts are symmetrically constructed, a Pozzo-Lucky incident in each preceding each time the appearance of the boy whose report is that Godot will not come today, 'but surely tomorrow'. The molecule of the play, its unit of effect, is symmetry, a symmetrical structure: the stage divided into two halves by the tree, the human race (so far as it is presented) divided into two, Didi and Gogo, then into four, Didi-Gogo and Pozzo-Lucky, then, with the boy's arrival, into two again, our sort, Godot's sort. And symmetries encompass opposites as well: Lucky's long speech in Act I, Lucky's utter silence in Act II. And symmetries govern the units of dialogue: at one extreme, the intricate fugue-like structure about the dead sounds and at the other extreme an exchange as short as this:

We could do our exercises.
Our movements.
Our relaxations.
Our elongations.
Our relaxations.
To warm us up.
To calm us down.
Off we go.

Or even as short as this:

How time flies when one has fun!

—three words and three words, pivoted on a 'when', and 'flies' alliterated with the incongruous 'fun'.

For nothing satisfies the mind like balance; nothing has so convincing a look of being substantial. The mind recoils from the random. That 'honesty is the best policy' seems a self-evident truth chiefly because the words are of metrical equivalence: honesty, policy. Proverbs work like that; sentences, even, work like that, and it is only by a difficult effort of attention, or else by the custom of the Civil Service, that a sentence with no balance can be constructed. Venture to utter a subject, and you will find your mind making ready a predicate that shall balance it. That is why we so seldom ask if lines of poetry make sense: the satisfactions of symmetry intervene. 'To be or not to be, that is the question', or: 'Tomorrow and tomorrow and tomorrow . . .' or: 'The cloud capp'd towers, the gorgeous palaces . . .'—such things derive much authority from equilibrium, and: 'In Xanadu did Kubla Khan . . .' exudes magic from its inversion of vowel sequence, -an, -u, -u, -an, despite our uncertainty about three of its five words. Beckett spent much time in his youth with the great virtuoso of such effects, James Joyce, whose last work, a sceptic's model of the universe, may be described as a system of intricate verbal recurrences to none of which a denotative meaning can with any confidence be assigned. And Laurel and Hardy would have been an utterly unconvincing couple were it not for the virtual identity of their hats, two shiny black bowlers.

It is rather from the second act of *Waiting for Godot* than from the first that its finest verbal symmetries can be culled, for the play converges on symmetry:

Say, I am happy.
I am happy.
So am I.
So am I.
We are happy.
We are happy. (*Silence.*) What do we do, now that we are happy?
Wait for Godot. (*Estragon groans. Silence.*)

The play also converges on certain very stark statements, the eloquence of which has sometimes left the impression that they are what the play 'means'. Thus Pozzo's 'They give birth astride of a grave, the light gleams an instant, then it's night once more', has manifested an unlucky quotability. It is wrung out of Pozzo, in the play, by Didi's pestiferous questioning. The last straw, elicited by the discovery that Lucky, who spoke so eloquently in Act I, is 'dumb' in Act II, has been the question,

'Dumb! Since when?'. Whereupon Pozzo ('*suddenly furious*') bursts out:

Have you not done tormenting me with your accursed time! It's abominable! When! When! One day, is that not enough for you, one day he went dumb, one day I went blind, one day we'll go deaf, one day we were born, one day we shall die, the same day, the same second, is that not enough for you? (*Calmer.*) They give birth astride of a grave, the light gleams an instant, then it's night once more. (*He jerks the rope.*) On!

This is to say, as so many things are to say, that we cannot be sure the play's two days are successive; to say that there are many days like these, that all waiting is endless, and all journeying. The striking metaphor is like Pozzo, that connoisseur of rhetoric. It sticks in Didi's mind, and a few minutes later, alone with the sleeping Gogo, he is reflecting that he too may be sleeping, so dream-like is the tedium.

Tomorrow, when I wake, or think I do, what shall I say of to-day? That with Estragon my friend, at this place, until the fall of night, I waited for Godot? That Pozzo passed, with his carrier, and that he spoke to us? Probably. But in all that what truth will there be?

Then he repeats the figure Pozzo used:

Astride of a grave and a difficult birth. Down in the hole, lingeringly, the grave-digger puts on the forceps. We have time to grow old. The air is full of our cries. (*He listens.*) But habit is a great deadener. (*He looks again at Estragon.*) At me too someone is looking, of me too someone is saying, He is sleeping, he knows nothing, let him sleep on. (*Pause.*) I can't go on! (*Pause.*) What have I said?

This is rather an aesthetic than a didactic climax, as the force and beauty of the language should indicate, and the strange figure of serial watchers. Didi is watching Gogo, we in the auditorium are watching Didi (though not saying that he is sleeping), someone invisible watches us all in turn: this evokes less a Deity than an infinite series. Like music, Beckett's language is shaped into phrases, orchestrated, cunningly repeated.

The statements it makes have torque within the work's context and only there, while the form, the symmetry, ministers to the form of the work, its wholeness, its uniqueness. We find other, quite different things said in quite different plays and novels of Beckett's, never wildly optimistic things it is true, but never ambitious of reaching outside the structure in which they are contained. It is that structure, shaped, sometimes self-cancelling if it pleases him, that he has laboured to perfect, draft after draft. And like all of us he has habitual attitudes. After years of familiarity with his work, I find no sign that it has ambitions to enunciate a philosophy of life. Nor had Stan Laurel.

2   Early life and poems

En attendant Godot made its author famous, as the phrase
goes, overnight. Or not quite overnight: word took a little time
to get around, and so did the play. It was published in October
1952, about three years after it had been written, and first
performed at the Théâtre de Babylone in Paris the following
January. The author's English version was published in 1954,
performed in Great Britain in 1955, and finally brought before
American audiences in 1956.

All this time rumour had been circulating about a play whose
title character didn't come, and while runs in the English-
speaking world tended to be short, reviewers baffled and audiences small, the title quickly became conversational currency:
conversational small change, in fact, apt to turn up in nightclub
routines, novels, commentaries. *Waiting for Godot:* like *The
Waste Land* a generation previously, those three words make
a time's emblem. Waiting, and not sure what you were waiting
for—a deliverance, a disaster, or simply for something to happen:
it was understood that the texture of contemporary experience
was like that. Some day a wise sociologist may see how to go
about explicating those tacit agreements to adopt a slogan.
It had valency if you knew nothing at all about the play, and
seemed to draw special force from the fact that next to nothing
was known about the author, whom no one succeeded in in-
terviewing, who was not photographed, who seemed not even
to answer mail. He was understood to be Irish, and to live
in Paris, where for some reason he insisted on writing in French.
He was also said to have had something to do with Joyce.

As knowledge goes this was not much, and fancy soon made
the inevitable surmise that he was a great pessimist, too gloomy
to speak. There were rumours of a new play in which he had
expressed his opinion of the human race by placing actors in
refuse bins. There were also said to be novels, pessimistic likewise. English versions of these began to appear in 1955, and
the fact that almost the whole first half of *Molloy* was one huge
paragraph seemed to verify another suspicion, that his work
was automatic writing, disdaining revision. This hypothesis
also served to account for a certain wavering in the narrative's
progression. Pessimist or no, automatic writer or no (both
notions were contested), he had anyhow given the decade its
label. In the 1950s we Waited for Godot.

The play would have been just as pertinent to the 1930s,
another decade of waiting. People with memories of that
dreary time remember how it was to be waiting year by year
for the next war. When that decade began Samuel Beckett
was twenty-three, and unnoticed though he had begun to
publish in magazines. When it ended, the war in progress at
last, he was still unnoticed though he had published four books
in four genres and been a continuing presence in the Paris
avant-garde.

He had come from an atypical Irish family—Protestant in
a Catholic country, modestly affluent in a poor country—and
had undertaken one of the Irish modes of suicide, which is
continental exile. That was not how he planned it, that was
what it became. What he had first intended was the academic
career so many twentieth-century men of letters have proposed.

His father, who was to leave an estate of £42,395, spent his
working days doing arithmetic, a window on reality many
Beckett protagonists were later to cherish. William Beckett
prospered as a quantity surveyor, estimator of the bricks and
man-hours some piece of construction would entail. Cool-
drinagh, the home he acquired in Foxrock south of Dublin,
was one measure of a self-made man's success, and his young-
est son Samuel distinguished himself at the best schools: Earls-
fort House School in Dublin, Portora Royal in the north,

Trinity College. His father's love of sports rubbed off on him, and his mother's piety, though he lost its convictions, never left his mind. He has recalled his childhood as a happy one. Nevertheless he had 'little talent for happiness', and much sensitivity to suffering. Before long he was unable to share his mother's belief that the Divine Will orders everything for the best. There was simply too much misery in the world. A girl he loved, for instance, died at twenty-four, coughing her lungs out.

He took his degree at Trinity in the spring of 1928, spent the next two years as an exchange student at the École Normale in Paris, and in 1930, having written a book on Proust, commenced teaching at Trinity. His lectures are said to have been long sonatas of structured silence, bounded and punctuated by low-voiced utterance. The post at Trinity seemed the fulfilment of many years' diligent costly preparation: his family's investment in the young man's intellectual promise, his own meticulous acquisition of languages and learning. Scholarship, teaching, these seemed clearly his destiny. At the end of the 1931 fall term, on a visit to relatives in Germany, he sent back to Trinity a letter of abrupt resignation. Inexplicably, he simply had to do it. So commenced the vagabond years.

Friends and family felt betrayed. Sam for his part felt he had betrayed them. Nevertheless he had discerned no choice. The classroom was simply not his life. An act of negation, straining loyalties; an act for which moreover no structure of reasons could be assigned: it was a paradigmatic Beckett event. We must be careful not to ponder the romance of the *acte gratuit*. It appears to be one of Beckett's deepest convictions that to actions of any import no reasons can really be assigned, except retrospectively, or for the sake of argument. We often find his characters arraying arguments. Being specious, their reasoning yields rich comedy. The mysteriousness at the heart of the action remains.

He dropped into nothingness. 'I lost the best', he has said, and he spent the next years not knowing what to do. Eighteen months later his father was dead of a heart attack. Sam Beckett spent two miserable years (1933-5) in London and six months wandering in Germany before he settled in Paris in the fall of 1936. Paris has been his home ever since.

Though his first published writing (1929) was a contribution to a symposium on Joyce, Beckett has published very little criticism and contributed little, and that little diffidently, to theoretical discussion of the art he practises. In the early years he mostly wrote poems and stories, many of which lie in periodical backfiles where their author judges they may as well remain. A few of the stories will be detaining us, only because they have lately been reprinted. The author's consent to this was extremely reluctant, and the British reprint was *hors commerce*. The poems in *Echo's Bones* (1936) seem to constitute the only early work he values at all. They may be found in *Poems in English* (London, 1961; New York, 1963). Written just before and just after the vagabond years commenced, they preserve complex hermetic miseries.

They are strangely frozen poems: a day fixed, a mood fixed, as it were for later thawing. Later work has drawn on them repeatedly. Early stories appropriated actual stretches of their wording; mature plays and fictions transpose their often obliquely stated situations, but sublimated, tranquillized. In the poems image follows image with a kind of violence which we may guess only the tranquillity of sublimation renders tolerable to him through the long process of conceiving and revising an extensive writing. What the poems cost him, how alarming he still found their energies twenty years later, may perhaps be judged from a novel he began about 1955. It employs the most consistent of all the situations in *Echo's Bones,* a blind cathartic journey through the Irish landscape:

Up bright and early that day, I was young then, feeling awful, and out, mother hanging out of the window in her nightdress weeping and waving. Nice fresh morning, bright too early as so often. Feeling really awful, very violent. The sky would soon darken and the rain fall and go on falling, all day, till evening. . . .

This recalls, for instance, the opening of 'Enueg I':[1]

Exeo in a spasm
tired of my darling's red sputum
from the Portobello Private Nursing Home
its secret things
and toil to the crest of the surge of the steep perilous bridge
and lapse down blankly under the scream of the hoarding
round the bright stiff banner of the hoarding
into a black west
throttled with clouds. . . .

The prose of 1955 retains and even amplifies the violent revulsions he put into the verse of 1931. He wrote thirteen more pages of prose, could not stay with the novel, yet could not jettison its opening either. He published it as *From an Abandoned Work*.

Unlike his mature writing, which speaks to numerous readers though Beckett himself is apt to be blank about it, the poems are apt to leave a reader blank though for Beckett they fix circumstantial memories: old crises and avulsions of the psyche, tied to times and landscapes. Applying a deft ice-pick with the author's generous help, Professor Lawrence E. Harvey (*Samuel Beckett, Poet and Critic,* Princeton, 1970) extracted and put on record the most extensive array of facts we have about Beckett's early life. None of his other writing is entangled with his biography in so specific a way, and unless we are informed we often catch only the tone of negation. Thus 'Enueg II' commences:

world world world world
and the face grave
cloud against evening

'Enueg I' suggests, and Professor Harvey confirms, that the face is a dead girl's. She died at twenty-four, and because of her green eyes and her fondness for wearing green she is remembered in early prose writings as Smeraldina ('little emerald'). 'Grave'—the word for her face—carries mortuary overtones as well as a demeanour of gravity. The face comes

> too late to darken the sky
> blushing away into the evening
> shuddering away like a gaffe

—as though her life had been a mistake the Creator retracted. We also read

> de morituris nihil nisi

—'of the dying nothing except . . . ': except what? Except everything? Is all our discourse of the dead or of the dying? In the vision of these poems it would seem so. The phantom face in the sky evokes the image of Christ's face that was imprinted on St Veronica's veil after she had wiped his brow on the *via dolorosa*:

> veronica mundi
> veronica munda
> give us a wipe for the love of Jesus

Bitterness wells up into word-play: 'mundi', of the world; 'munda', neat and clean: neat lady-saint, the world's wiper. So the speaker—

> sweating like Jesus
> tired of dying
> tired of policemen

—is trudging to crucifixion, and the policemen, who won't let a man lie down on the pavement, resemble centurions. Eventually he does lie down for a while, on O'Connell Street's great bridge,

> goggling at the tulips of the evening
> the green tulips
> shining round the corner like an anthrax
> shining on Guinness's barges

Elements of this poem become themes in Beckett's later work. The plight of a man haunted by a lost girl's face ('The face in the ashes/That old starlight/On the earth again') is at the centre

of the 1962 radio play, *Words and Music.* The man who com-
pares himself to Christ is like Gogo in *Waiting for Godot* ('All
my life I've compared myself to him'). The man whose agitated
life is an endless journeying, a *via crucis* interrupted only by
episodes of collapse, will become Molloy, Moran, Malone,
Macmann, Mahood, all those weary journeyers of the novels.
In these works the themes and situations need no commentary,
so direct and so untrammeled is their eloquence. In the poem,
however, the tics of a nervous verbal energy keep distracting
us, and when we have disengaged the themes they may lie numb
unless we have biographical facts for context. Thus 'sweating
like Judas' seems a pointless bit of irritation until we learn
that Beckett wrote 'Enueg II' late in 1931, when the resolve
to resign from Trinity and so 'betray' family and colleagues
was taking form in his mind. 'Like a gaffe' similarly seems an
empty gesture until we are assured that the face in the sky
betokens a life so unlucky it should never have been commenced.

Many of the poems in *Echo's Bones* are like that. The emotions they assert exceed the realized situations they produce,
emotions we can understand when we know more than the
poems tell us. Similar emotions will justify themselves when
they arise from the produced situations of the plays and novels,
attached to just such symbols—the journey, the collapse, the
anguished waiting—as the poems sketch and hint at but do
not constate.

How to work in the very brief time of a poem, making its
elements cohere as well as suggest, was a craft he was to learn.
He achieved it at least once in *Echo's Bones,* in the poem called
'The Vulture'; in later poems, notably several in French, he
was to achieve it again and again. The successful poems grow
very quietly in the mind, earning their strangely gentle apocalypse.
'Saint-Lô (1946) is a poem the mind's apprehensions may at
first be too clumsy to pick up, but in time it can teach a sub-
missive dexterity.

SAINT-LÔ

Vire will wind in other shadows

unborn through the bright ways tremble
and the old mind ghost-forsaken
sink into its havoc

We may feel that it says nothing apprehensible. Still, the opening modulation, 'Vire will wind' (Vire is the river of Saint-Lô)
solicits the memory repeatedly, until we pick up, perhaps,
the echo of 'wind' in 'mind', and then think to apply the mind's
'havoc' to the ruins of the war-beaten city, and associate
'shadows' and 'ghosts', and gradually grow familiar with the
tiny structure: two lines about Saint-Lô, two lines about the
speaker, the halves of the poem, by a baffling geometry, at
once parallel and divergent. Cities, its theme runs, are renewed
like rivers; men die. The Vire is a Heraclitean stream with a
future of self-renewal; and the bombed city too will be rebuilt
and cast shadows again. The mind, however, this mind, unlike
the river will grow old, and will 'sink' (an oddly apt water-word),
and its 'havoc' unlike the city's will precede no second rising.

The syntax of the second line floats richly. Does 'unborn'
go with 'shadows' and say they are not born yet? Or with 'Vire',
and say that categories of temporal origin are inappropriate
to a river, even to the future river? Or does unborn stand ab-
solutely, positing 'the unborn', men still to be born and one
day to 'tremble' spirit-like in what will be 'bright ways'? This
lucid indeterminacy is like water. The poem works with Beckett's normal unit of thought, a sentence of perhaps two dozen
words, scrupulously interwoven.

And it is self-contained, though not quite. Every verbal
structure, however turned-in and patterned, draws on the world
beyond it for the meanings of its words, and on the past for
the spells its words can cast. So we need to know that Vire
is the river of Saint-Lô, and such verbal sensitivities as we may
have acquired reinforce the poem too, prompting us for instance
to recognize in 'ghost' an intensification of one overtone of
'shadow'. We do not need, however, the kind of private information for lack of which so many details in *Echo's Bones*
go blank: in this case the knowledge that Beckett's life was
involved with Saint-Lô for some months commencing late

in 1945, when he was interpreter and storekeeper at the Red Cross Hospital amongst its ruins.

A final example, from 1948:

> *je suis ce cours de sable qui glisse*
> *entre le galet et la dune*
> *la pluie d'été pleut sur ma vie*
> *sur moi ma vie qui me fuit me poursuit*
> *et finira le jour de son commencement*
>
> *cher instant je te vois*
> *dans ce rideau de brume qui recule*
> *où je n'aurai plus à fouler ces longs seuils mouvants*
> *et vivrai le temps d'une porte*
> *qui s'ouvre et se referme*

In Beckett's English:

> my way is in the sand flowing
> between the shingle and the dune
> the summer rain rains on my life
> on me my life harrying fleeing
> to its beginning to its end
>
> my peace is there in the receding mist
> when I may cease from treading these long shifting thresholds
> and live the space of a door
> that opens and shuts

Once more the melancholy is structured: shifting sand underfoot, a path bounded by two worlds, the world of dead dunes, the world of cold recurring water; and rain on the journeyer, mist surrounding him. These draw for their eloquence on traditional usage: the sands of time, the journey of life, the journeyer beset left and right by extremes, futurity as a curtain,[2] death as a door. The door opens and closes like the mist, a kind of continous door. As he moves along the sand, mist opens before him, closes behind him. Time is a seamless flow of penetration, the present instant passing out of mystery into mystery, and one may hope (*'cher instant je te vois'*) for some decisive moment, a demarked door through which to pass,

a door that will decisively close. How thoroughly traditional
such images are! Beckett's images normally are. But normally
too, as when the 'long shifting thresholds' introduce that surprising door on the strand, he achieves a pairing of traditional
images as bizarre as a Magritte painting. For imagine, as
the poem half-incites us to imagine, a wooden portal, empty,
mist-enshrouded, standing alone on that beach.

And how little the poem *insists*. It implies a calm low voice,
a refusal of emphasis. If we look back to the early poems we
find them sharply insisting, telling phenomena that try the
nerves: green tulips shining like anthrax, feet in marmalade.
It was an exacerbated, not a composed energy that thrust such
insistences into those poems, poems whose only theme was
that life in a universe of death assaults the nerves intolerably.

3   Early stories

From *A Dream of Fair to Middling Women,* an unpublished
episodic novel of 1932, still preserved and occasionally shown
to friends, Beckett extrapolated ten interlocked stories, published in 1934 as *More Pricks Than Kicks.* When he was famous
his publishers wanted to reissue it, and he gave way at length
most reluctantly. He was right to be reluctant. The book will
chiefly interest students. With carefully directed attention, we
can perceive latent in it his later directions. Other claims should
not be made.

Joyce in those years was deep into his *Work in Progress,*
and the young Beckett's title bears a Joycean stamp. 'Saul,
Saul, why persecutest thou me?' a voice out of blinding light
said to Saul on the road to Damascus. 'It is hard for thee to
kick against the pricks.' (Acts xxvi. 14). The 'prick' (a goad)
is driving Christ's reluctant ox down the road to apostleship.
Such voices from his Protestant upbringing would have come
often to the young Beckett in his Bohemian years, and in his
book's title the pricks are phallic, the kicks are eroticism's
sparse rewards: a compelled Bohemianism, he seems to say,
with less fun in it than you'd think.

Numerous women bring Beckett's hero little fun. Their
sexual importunities are especially alarming. The life of his
hero, Belacqua, is the life of a looker-on, the active pricks
those of other men on whose woodland trysts he spies. In one
story, 'Walking Out', we find Lucy, his betrothed, understandably disapproving of this recreation. Belacqua hopes
that by the time they are married she will have taken a paramour

and left him to his own delectations, their married life thus established 'on this solid basis of cuckoldry'. She will not hear of it. She has orthodox cravings, from the depredations of which he is saved by an accident that cripples her sexual system. So their marriage, till she died two years later, was happy according to Belacqua's lights. They sat up to all hours playing the gramophone, and he found 'in her big eyes better worlds than this'. It is a typical story in its perverse refusal to observe any norms of behaviour story-readers expect.

Belacqua Shuah's perversity starts with his name—no more improbable a name in Dublin, come to think of it, than Stephen Dedalus. He is named for the lazy old friend Dante encountered in ante-Purgatory (*Purg*. iv, 97-135), 'lazier than if Sloth were his very sister', and waiting in the shadow of a rock till as many years shall have passed as he lived on earth: the perfect type, for Beckett, of a man reliving his whole life at a remove. In the first story Belacqua is introduced as a student of Dante, 'stuck in the first of the canti in the moon', and no reader who consults Beatrice's explanation of why the moon has dark patches (*Par*. ii, 52-148) will find his difficulties surprising. Beckett's story, 'Dante and the Lobster', contains a tacit analogy between the dark patches on the moon and the existence of suffering on earth. The dark patches, and Beatrice's rationalizing, represent an intellectual exercise for Belacqua. Street gossip about a condemned man's last day he receives with comparable detachment. But the fate of a lobster ('My God, it's alive') overwhelms him. 'But it's not dead, you can't boil it like that.' His aunt bids him have sense. '"Lobsters are always boiled alive. They must be." She caught up the lobster and laid it on its back. It trembled. "They feel nothing" she said.' But Belacqua cannot detach himself from its plight.

In the depths of the sea it had crept into the cruel pot. For hours, in the midst of its enemies, it had breathed secretly. It had survived the Frenchwoman's cat and his witless clutch. Now it was going alive into scalding water. It had to. Take into the air my quiet breath.

There is no stay of execution. It will drop into the boiling water like a soul into—purgatory, perhaps? Extinction?

　She lifted the lobster clear of the table. It had about thirty seconds
to live.
　Well, thought Belacqua, it's a quick death, God help us all.
　It is not.

No, it is not, not so far as one can imagine, and from this first
and best of the stories in *More Pricks Than Kicks* that terminal
sentence reverberates in the memory. No Beckett death is quick.
All Beckett lives are dyings. Some of the dying contrive to
ignore this fact. Women especially ignore it, and woman
after woman comes crashing through the walls of Belacqua's
solipsism, athirst to woo him into union and procreation.
In 'Fingal' he eludes one of them by mad pedalling on a stolen
bicycle. In 'Love and Lethe' a suicide pact with another goes
awry: they make love instead, female will being indestructible.
Or not quite indestructible; a collision between her horse
and a motor-car interdicts the bride he takes in 'Walking Out'
from sharing anything with him but gramophone music. The
second bride he takes in 'What a Misfortune' perishes of 'sun-
set and honeymoon'. In 'Yellow' nurses beset him as he awaits
minor surgery; he dies under anaesthesia in the story's casual
ending, and in the last story, 'Draff', his third wife is forming
a new liaison with a man disposed to appreciate physicality.
('He grappled with the widow, he simply could not help it.
She was a sensible girl in some ways, she was not ashamed to
let herself go in the arms of a man of her own weight at last.
They broke away, carrot plucked from tin of grease.') Their
last service to Belacqua is to cushion his grave with moss,
fern and turf. It is possible to imagine him happy there.
　Adrift, beset, holding futile conversations with relentless
girls whose territory is the physical world, Belacqua is a first
sketch for the heroes of Beckett's mature fictions, bumping
round in a cosmos where nothing synchronizes nor harmonizes.
The intended point of the stories is an elaborate pointlessness, a theme for which Beckett at that time did not possess
the technique. The normal world of fiction is a tidy world,

neatly summarized by a Jesuit in 'A Wet Night' who has the
last word in an argument by demonstrating the causalities
of leaving a bus:

'Observe' he said, 'I desire to get down. I pull this cord and the bus
stops and lets me down. . . . In just such a Gehenna of links' said
this remarkable man, with one foot on the pavement, 'I forged my
vocation.'

'A Gehenna of links', that is the religious view; no sparrow
falls without cause. It is also the principle of normal fiction,
and moreover the fiction-reader's expectation of the normal
world. Motives should be explicit, persons should be comple-
mentary or else antithetical, purposes should comply. Beckett
in his twenties devoted to such assumptions an energy of de-
struction that transcends any desire to reform fiction and
can only be explained by the fact that they are religious assumptions as well. He exhausted on fiction his outrage at being
told, for instance by preachers, that everything comports
and harmonizes in a world which the Divine Purpose permeates
as the novelist's purpose permeates a novel. A 1938 poem,
'Ooftish' (*Auf dem Tisch*: put your money down) declines to
be persuaded that human suffering makes transcendental sense
when knowingly invested. 'Offer it up plank it down,' speaks
a caricature of the religious voice, 'cancer angina it is all one
to us cough up your T.B. don't be stingy.' He once heard
a sermon like that, in Ireland; the poem ends with a bitter
summation of its drift:

> so parcel up the whole issue and send it along
> the whole misery diagnosed undiagnosed misdiagnosed
> get your friends to do the same we'll make use of it
> we'll make sense of it we'll put it in the pot with the rest
> it all boils down to the blood of the lamb

That is, so to speak, God the Novelist speaking, a Purpose
for whom all misery makes ultimate sense. But it makes no
sense, Beckett habitually protested. Transferring his protest
to the critique of fiction, he asserted in 1931[3] his preference
for characters who 'will not suffer their systems to be absorbed

in the cluster of a greater system', and who moreover themselves 'tend to disappear as systems', feeling no obligation to appear coherent. People have, it is true, moments of 'backwash' when they seem to cohere, and normal fictionists—Balzac, Jane Austen—focus on this 'nervous recoil into composure' as though it much mattered, because in its throes the characters are tractable.

To read Balzac is to receive the impression of a chloroformed world. He is absolute master of his material, he can do what he likes with it, he can foresee and calculate its least vicissitude, he can write the end of his book before he has finished the first paragraph, because he has turned all his creatures into clock-work cabbages and can rely on their staying put wherever needed or staying going at whatever speed in whatever direction he chooses. The whole thing, from beginning to end, takes place in a spellbound backwash. . .

He also wrote that the reality of the individual 'is an incoherent reality and must be expressed incoherently', a dangerous way of putting it. Then and later, he had more sense than to write incoherently. His mature works, constantly evading paraphrase, are marvels of suave coherence attained on the plane of syntax and idiom. His early fictions attempted a double strategy. They asserted incoherence by teasing the reader with centripetal cleverness, the foreground filled with epigram, dramatic events passed over in asides, or beneath allusions.[4] They sought to order incoherence by containing anticlimax within our expectations of climax, relying on the reader to supply, often with heroic resilience, the contours of the familiar story the author is refusing to write. That is an unsatisfactory method, to be sure, presuming as it does the viability of the archtypes you are refuting, but it will do, if you are a young writer, while you work out a better one.

We can most readily see Beckett doing this in 'A Wet Night', the longest story in *More Pricks Than Kicks,* toward the end of which we realize that we are reading a parody of the longest story in *Dubliners,* 'The Dead'. The Christmas party is there, the numerous company, the fatuous talk, the return of a couple home. And to ensure that we identify the prototype, a specific passage is parodied too, as we shall see.

Now Joyce's stories pertain, exactly, to 'a chloroformed world'. His own word was 'paralysis'. Dublin, he wrote to a prospective publisher, was 'the centre of Irish paralysis', and readers might be willing to pay, he hoped, 'for the special odour of corruption which floats over my stories'. Like thick brown varnish on a genre painting, that psychic corruption harmonizes everything. People move, think, talk predictably, and Joyce's stories are tidy, economical, devoid of loose ends and accidental phrases.

Beckett's point in parodying 'The Dead' was not to expose the master he revered as a charlatan: rather, to emphasize the relationship between tonal unity and a world in which nothing unexpected can really happen. Through Joyce's famous terminal setpiece about falling snow we understand how nature's least purposive gesture, the very weather of a Dublin winter night, rhymes with the uniform inevitability of human stasis: the wife asleep with her memories, the husband gazing at the gathering whiteness which levels and unifies all phenomena: a certain grave in Galway, and the mountains, and the city, and the air, and all Dubliners, and 'the dark mutinous Shannon waves'. This is the passage to which Beckett keys his finale.

Belacqua sees his girl home from the party in a taxi (she pays, since he spent his last penny on a bottle), and they go inside, to experience more amusing diversions than Gabriel and Gretta Conroy did: 'the bottle, some natural tears[5] and in what hair he had left her high-frequency fingers.' Meanwhile it begins 'to rain again upon the earth', and the parody, keyed by Joycean mannerisms like the word 'epiphany' and a word like the thunder-word in *Work in Progress*, gets under way in earnest. The prose adopts a temporarily suave texture:

But the wind had dropped, as it so often does in Dublin when all the respectable men and women whom it delights to annoy have gone to bed, and the rain fell in a uniform untroubled manner. It fell upon the bay, the littoral, the mountains and the plains, and mostly upon the Central Bog it fell with a rather desolate uniformity.

Part of the anticlimax is not to sustain this. Part, again, is not
to let it end the story. His spirits blanketed not by the precip-
itation as Gabriel Conroy's were, but by drink and fatigue and
constitutional psychic nausea, Belacqua creeps out, throws his
boots away because they hurt him, doubles up with 'such a
belly-ache as he had never known', makes his way homeward
'with his poor trunk parallel to the horizon', collapses to the
pavement, and makes shift to investigate with drunken pertinacity the movements of his hands before his face; whereupon
a policeman's voice 'enjoined him to move on, which, the pain
being so much better, he was only too happy to do.'

This is not a brilliant ending, but a symptomatic gesture:
a rejection of the unified polyphonic resolution. Dante's Belacqua may be imagined re-dreaming his life in the lifetime's
hours that he has beside that rock. Later a Beckett protagonist
so aged his years have left Belacqua's rioting far behind will
revisit as it were the life of Beckett's Belacqua, and like him
terminate a fiction by simply collapsing ('Molloy could stay,
where he happened to be.'). Next, in the second part of *Molloy,*
a kind of policeman will go in search of him, and more or less
turn into him; next, in *Malone Dies,* in a further incarnation
he will die like Belacqua in what seems to be a kind of nursing-
home; next, in a last embodiment (if we are still to speak of
bodies) *The Unnamable* will speak endlessly from beyond bodily
death. And Beckett in the 1930s drafted a story called 'Echo's
Bones' in which the dead Belacqua like his prototype in Dante
revisits a life in which he had contrived to pass the greater
share of his time 'in the privy, papered in ultraviolet anguish,
of my psyche.' We may say that this story, never published,
became *The Unnamable.*

In 1934, when he published *More Pricks Than Kicks*, this
remarkable trio of fictions lay far in the future. When it should
be achieved, then the impulse behind the early stories would
at last be laid to rest. Meanwhile he had a more immediate
project, which was to try not a parody of standard fiction,
but the expedient of surrounding an unassimilable hero with
characters who are caught up in a standard fiction. He was

living in London, and the hero he was excogitating, also exiled in London, would sojourn in the privy of his psyche and hope that his ashes' destiny might also be a privy. This was Murphy.

4 Murphy

Murphy, the work of a penniless man just past thirty, may be the first reader-participation novel. Fully to get the hang of it, you must set pieces on the board when you are part way through Chapter 11 and work out a chess game. You are advised to be vigilant earlier than that. Beckett has greatly enjoyed the game of tucking stray pieces of information into pockets whence only deduction can retrieve them. Thus the amplitude of Miss Counihan's buttocks is to be gathered from a sentence that does not mention them: 'I fear you would not pass through the door of my cupboard, not even sideways, not even frontways rather.' Thus one way of being sure that the year is 1935 is to note that 1936 is yet to come, that 1933, the year of the *Morro Castle* disaster, is in the past, and that 12 September falls on a Thursday. (Pursuing these trivia we may miss that Sunday, 4 October 1936, is 'a full year' ahead.)

Then there is information we seem to get but don't. The second paragraph of the book offers us Murphy 'naked in his rocking-chair of undressed teak' (an inconspicuous phrase, so plausible does 'undressed' look next to 'naked', though who would have made and even 'guaranteed' such a chair?), and he is tied to the chair by his own choice, and even by his own hand. (We guess that he habitually ties himself; later on our guess is confirmed.) Now:

Seven scarves held him in position. Two fastened his shins to the rockers, one his thighs to the seat, two his breast and belly to the back, one his wrists to the strut behind. Only the most local movements were possible.

Very good. Now: (1) where is the seventh scarf? (2) how was the sixth scarf tied? 'His wrists to the strut behind': the reader is invited to experiment.

This is not the only time we shall find Beckett lending his most careful descriptive techniques to delineating a situation that is quite impossible. In a later novel, *Watt*, a lengthy passage is devoted to the question how Watt moves from place to place by the use of his legs. Since Watt is not a man but a writer's creation, we may feel some little curiosity about this matter, but we may not expect the answer to have been so fully thought out:

Watt's way of advancing due east, for example, was to turn his bust as far as possible towards the north and at the same time to fling out his right leg as far as possible towards the south, and then to turn his bust as far as possible towards the south and at the same time to fling out his left leg as far as possible towards the north . . . . The knees, on these occasions, did not bend . . . . The arms were content to dangle, in perfect equipendency.

Very well then, that is how he chose to move about. But elsewhere we are given information about the coat Watt never takes off: it is a cloth cylinder, and the skirts are not divided. Bringing these pieces of information together, we find legs that are trammelled by an enclosing cylinder, and that are nevertheless flung towards points of the compass; and if Buster Keaton, say, could have perfected a way of walking similar to Watt's, he would have been hard put to demonstrate it while encased in such a coat.

A novel, in short, is a novel, not a map of the familiar world, and Beckett's novels differ from most in the consistency of their insistence upon this principle. If God wrote the script of the familiar world, he laid down also the principles that govern in it the possible and the impossible. Beckett's covert suggestion appears to be that these principles are as arbitrary as the rules of chess, which likewise state what is possible and impossible. An Aristotle, stating that two bodies cannot occupy the same space at the same time, is in the position of an observer of many

chess games, who has noticed that no player ever moves a rook
diagonally, and is finally confident to announce the law that
governs the rook's move. Though he can offer no *reason* why a
rook never moves diagonally, he can observe that in chess it
never does, and postulate that both players understand this, as
one of the conditions of undertaking a game. Now we can
imagine that there is no *reason* why a body cannot pass through
another body, except that such a thing is never observed; and
this is one of the understandings under which the games in God's
universe are played. The games in a novel are played in a different
universe, where for instance a man can place his hands behind
him and then tie his wrists securely to a strut on the back of his
chair. We do not see him do this, but we see that it has been done,
and since the novelist has nowhere undertaken to conform to
God's rules, we have no license to complain. On one occasion—
it is in *Watt* again—Beckett is quite specific about the principle
employed: 'Haemophilia is, like enlargement of the prostate,
an exclusively male disorder. But not in this work.'

The comedy arises from this, that the novelist employs the
language we all employ, a language human beings have devised
to conform with the world in which they have been placed.
It is odd to find, periodically, that this language, which by its
very nature seems adapted to setting forth illusions of the familiar,
has lent itself to transcriptions of the impossible, without a
ruffled surface, without so much as the equivalent of a lifted
eyebrow.

And the *Murphy* world is the world of the familiar. We are
in London, in West Brompton, in 1935, and it is moreover 12
September, a Thursday. The view is to the north-west, and we
may wonder incidentally why a north-west window needs to be
curtained off from the sun, since so meticulous a writer does
not put down 'sun' when he means 'daylight'. Or rather, if
the detail catches our attention, we are not to wonder but to
accept. This narrative insists on its own laws, close to those of
the great world but with unobtrusive gestures of dissent.

Murphy's own gestures of dissent are less unobtrusive, provided
one is privileged (as we are) to observe them. They include

tying himself naked into his chair and rocking until his body is 'appeased', after which, we are told, it will be possible for him to 'come alive in his mind, as described in section six'. 'And life in the mind gave him pleasure, such pleasure that pleasure was not the word,' so it is not surprising that he prefers not to have his means of achieving it discovered by a potential meddler, for instance 'his landlady . . . or some other lodger'. And there is danger of this, because the telephone starts to ring, and he cannot free a hand to answer it. 'His landlady or some other lodger', obedient to its summons as a Pavlov dog, may very well rush in to answer it. He struggles to free a hand, so as to answer it himself. When he does succeed, the caller is Celia.

Between the description of Murphy in the chair and the episode of the telephone, we learn in a flashback about a time before Celia, when Murphy's distraction was a Miss Counihan. In this flashback we encounter a sage named Neary, capable of stopping his heart at will, and partial to Pythagorean terminology. We learn from Neary's dialogue with Murphy that whereas Neary is capable of obsessed love, Murphy is not. We also learn that the dialogue in this novel is highly formal.

'The love that lifts up its eyes,' said Neary, 'being in torments; that craves for the tip of her little finger, dipped in lacquer, to cool its tongue—is foreign to you, Murphy, I take it.'

'Greek', said Murphy.

'Or put it another way,' said Neary; 'the single, brilliant, organized, compact blotch in the tumult of heterogeneous sensation.'

'Blotch is the word,' said Murphy.

Neary's first speech takes its terminology, all but the lacquer, from the parable of Dives and Lazarus (Luke xvi: 24); his second, from the psychology of William James, for whom the mind detached patterns from the big blooming buzzing confusion. And when he tells Murphy that Murphy is past saving—'I should say your conarium has shrunk to nothing' —he invokes the most curious detail in the philosophy of René Descartes, for whom the conarium, more popularly known as the pineal gland, was the location of the otherwise incomprehensible intercourse between the body and the mind. With a conarium shrunk to nothing, Murphy leads a completely dual existence, love assaulting his body only, while his mind strives to be free ('as described in section six').

Chapter 2 introduces Celia as a table of measurements, *i.e.* as a body *par excellence*. We learn of her first view of Murphy the previous June, considering alternately the sky and a star-chart. Murphy glimpsed her as his eyes were dropping from sky to chart, resolved to let his gaze linger on her during their next ascension from chart to sky, if she was still there; did gaze, 'for perhaps two minutes', an inspection encouraged by her rotating in his line of sight with outstretched arms; but did not subsequently move forward or speak. Rather, his eyes shut out this distracting vision, then 'the jaws clenched, the chin jutted, the knees sagged, the hypogastrium came forward, the mouth opened, the head tilted slowly back.' He resumed, in short, his inspection of the sky. It was love at first sight, nevertheless. 'Every moment that Celia spent away from Murphy seemed an eternity devoid of significance, and Murphy for his part expressed the same thought if possible more strongly in the words: "What is my life now but Celia?"' This is a less extravagant statement than it may seem, pertaining as it does only to the life he seeks to obliterate by his ritual of rocking.

Murphy belongs 'to no profession or trade', does nothing discernible, never rips up old stories (which suggests that he may somehow generate stories, and put them on paper, and constitutes our only hint that Murphy may attempt writing from time to time), and lives on 'small charitable sums', derived, it turns out, from an uncle to whom by arrangement the landlady submits cooked accounts. He declines to seek a job. 'He begged her to believe him when he said he could not earn. Had he not already sunk a small fortune in attempts to do so?' He is 'a chronic emeritus', and alleges that there are metaphysical considerations, moreover, 'in whose gloom it appeared that the night had come in which no Murphy could work.' A bum, a parasite, however periphrastically described, and

Celia understandably has left him. She will return when he undertakes to look for work.

This is familiar fictional stuff; in fact Celia's are the standard fictional motions and emotions. Murphy's are not, for we are not to suppose him lazy. He is simply devoid of incentive, being a dualist drawn to the life of the mind, and hence drawn away from work, which entails the exertions of the body. This is an odd premise for a book, but Beckett characteristically does hang his works on odd premises, usually philosophical ones. The whole of his one film script (called *Film*) is predicated on Bishop Berkeley's principle, *esse est percipi*. In a comedy extraneous to the film itself, we must imagine Buster Keaton and sundry technicians pondering this oracle at the head of the first page of the shooting script.

The Beckett novel or play or film, in fact, is strikingly similar to a non-Euclidean geometry. Euclid's geometry derives from five postulates, all of which strike commonsense as irrefutable, but one of which, the parallel postulate, has a long history of irritating mathematicians who feel it is somehow a little less self-evident than the other four. It states in effect that through a point only one line parallel to a given line can be drawn. Efforts have been made to get rid of this postulate by simply deducing it from the other four, which would turn it into a detail in the system, not a principle of the system. The repeated failure of such efforts is part of the history of mathematics, as is also the heroic next step of Lobachevsky; for, said Lobachevsky, if the parallel postulate is not self-evident, as appears from all the pother it has aroused, and if it is not entailed by the other four, as appears from the failure of all attempts to derive it from them, why, let us see what view of the geometrical world will ensue if we alter it. What if through a point *no* line can be drawn parallel to a given line?

There is no evident way of denying Lobachevsky's right to take this step. No one can test the parallel postulate, since to do so one would have to journey to infinity in order to verify whether the lines in question meet there or fail to meet. (All the other postulates can be verified right on the paper in front of us.)

So Lobachevsky elaborated a system in which no parallel lines were possible, and later systems were elaborated in which many parallel lines might all pass through the same point, and so far were such non-Euclidean systems from being empty games that Einstein incorporated one of them into his map of relativity's cosmos.

In the same way, says Beckett, let us assume that to be is to be perceived, and make a film. Or, let us assume that Godot will never come, and write *Waiting for Godot*. Or, let us assume that the mind may be bodytight, the body mindtight, in the sense in which we call a ship watertight; let us carry to a point of exquisite finality the intuitions man has long entertained about the separability of bodily and mental experience (and if we are to adopt the Cartesian terminology this will entail shrinking his pineal gland to zero), and accordingly let us write *Murphy*. Murphy will look like that familiar phenomenon, the shiftless man, and he will irritate Celia as if he were shiftless, but the reader will understand otherwise.

The man careless of the great world, the man indifferent to those concerns the right management of which constitutes the chief preoccupation of most novels, will recur and recur in Beckett's fictions. In later works this man will display less and less of Murphy's seedy gentility. He will be driven, obscurely, by irrational needs, forever on the move; he will be indistinguishable, to the outer eye, from what inhabitants of the great world have learned to call the tramp. The point of view of the fiction will approximate his, so that we shall not observe him with the outer eye, and shall have the unexpected sensation of finding the affairs of the great world—our own affairs—less than comprehensible. He will make no effort at liaison with the great world at all, or else feeble efforts, known to be foredoomed. Murphy makes a minimum effort: he leaves his dealings with the great world to the ministration of the stars, and is consequently preoccupied with horoscopes. The novel likewise, by its constant ritual of noting the position of the sun in the zodiac, conveys the impression that if the intricate doings of the characters are intelligible on any principle whatever, they are intelligible in

terms of some vast overarching interlocking system such as that
of the heavens. Certainly the overall design of the action yields
its symmetries only to detached inspection, the inspection that
makes plot-diagrams like horoscopes.

Murphy makes no effort to come to terms with the people
around him, their system of deeds and choices, but rather to
come to terms with the cosmic system of which, it is implied,
such deeds and choices constitute a subset. Insofar as the peopled
world impinges on his attention, his primary effort (Celia
usually excepted) is to withdraw from it. In this he differs from
the protagonists of the subsequent fictions, who see no hope of
withdrawing wholly from the peopled world, and struggle
instead to subsist in it. Insofar as the great world exacts from
Murphy some effort at coexistence, he follows a strategy, unique
to him, for coping with it always at one remove, consulting his
horoscope rather than what most of us call facts. When Tickle-
penny brings him, in Chapter 5, the opportunity to work in a
madhouse, Murphy leaps at the coincidence between 'lunatic'
in the second paragraph of his horoscope and 'custodian' in the
seventh. No more motivation is offered, or required.

The great world contains various busy conniving folk, notably
Neary, Wylie, Cooper, Miss Counihan. It is regulated by
interest and appetite, notably sexual appetite, and it is the
domain proper to traditional novels because it is characterized
by an endless round of *transactions*, fit to be diagrammed as
though by Newton or a seminar tutor. A desires the favours of
B, who however is enamoured of C, who is turned toward D.
Linking and unlinking these various attachments by means of
enhancing or diminishing the desirability in A's eyes of B,
or in D's of C, will constitute a 'plot', and these enhancings
and diminishments will reflect fluctuating estimates of value,
i.e. of status and fortune. Values have been arbitrarily assigned
to the pieces, and when the foreordained combinations have
been achieved—for instance King of Hearts with Queen of
Hearts—the plot will be 'resolved'.

This paradigmatic 'novel' hovers in the background, super-
intending our sense of what goes on among grotesque ciphers.

Thus in Chapter 4, Neary has loved Miss Counihan ever since February, but Miss Counihan's affections are inexplicably set on Murphy, whom she supposes to be making a success of himself in London. To disengage her dreams from Murphy, it will suffice to produce proof that he is not an 'aspirant to fiscal distinction' but a shiftless bum. To this end Neary dispatches Cooper to London. But Cooper fails; whereupon Wylie, who also aspires to Miss Counihan ('What a bust!' he exclaims. 'All centre and no circumference!') proposes that Neary also go to London in quest of Murphy, while he, Wylie, sees to the maintenance of Miss Counihan's passions. By Chapter 7, Wylie has established himself in Miss Counihan's breast, and has a personal stake in disengaging her from Murphy. For this purpose he and she also head for London.

All of this is as pointless as it sounds. These chapters depend on Beckett's talent, early nourished, for so heightening the dialogue as to give the transactions among his cartoon figures a look of philosophical sanction. Thus his talkers invoke the principle of compensation: whenever a piece is moved it leaves a gap behind it, to be filled by another piece; every choice entails a relinquishment as well as a fulfilment; the system's supply of potential energy is constant. (This might also mean that satisfactions are in equilibrium, so that it doesn't matter what you do, but the Wylies and Nearys do not draw such a conclusion, economical of energy though it would prove.) The notion is one with which Beckett often plays. In *Godot*, 'The tears of the world are a constant quantity. For each one who begins to weep somewhere else another stops. The same is true of the laugh.' And in *Murphy*, 'The syndrome known as life is too diffuse to admit of palliation. For every symptom that is eased, another is made worse. The horse leech's daughter is a closed system. Her quantum of wantum cannot vary.' ('"Very prettily put," said Neary.') And again:

  'From all of which I am to infer,' said Neary, 'correct me if I am wrong, that the possession—*Deus det!*—of angel Counihan will create an aching void to the same amount.'

And:

'I declare to my God,' said Neary, 'sometimes you talk as great tripe as Murphy.'

'Once a certain degree of insight has been reached,' said Wylie, 'all men talk, when talk they must, the same tripe.'

Murphy's attachment meanwhile is to Celia, who does not talk tripe, except insofar as her insistence that he find work may be described as tripe. She is, on this side, one more cartoon figure, the Nagging Fiancée, and Murphy, preposterously seeking work, a cartoon figure himself likewise.

Goaded by the thought of losing Celia even were it only by night (for she had promised not to 'leave' him any more), Murphy applied at a chandlery in Gray's Inn Road for the position of smart boy, fingering his lemon bow nervously . . . .

The chandlers all came galloping out to see the smart boy.

''E ain't smart,' said the chandler, 'not by a long chork 'e ain't.'

'Nor 'e ain't a boy,' said the chandler's semi-private convenience, 'not to my mind 'e ain't.'

''E don't look rightly human to me,' said the chandlers' eldest waste product, 'not rightly.'

Murphy was too familiar with this attitude of derision tinged with loathing to make the further blunder of trying to abate it. Sometimes it was expressed more urbanely, sometimes less. Its forms were as various as the grades of the chandler mentality, its content was one: 'Thou surd!'

Celia, nagging, displays the Chandler Mentality. But Celia is also—an anomaly in this work—a sympathetic human being. She is wistful and distressed; she can not merely be put to slapstick inconvenience, she can be hurt. When Cooper in Chapter 7 finds Murphy only to lose him, it is slapstick hide-and-seek; when Celia in the same chapter, troubled by Murphy's absence (he has taken the madhouse job) wanders off of Hyde Park to watch her uncle Willoughby Kelly flying his kite and does not find him there, an unfamiliar mood proves to be suffusing the novel, that of elegiac disappointment.

She sat on till it was nearly dark and all the flyers, except the child, had gone. At last he also began to wind in and Celia watched for the kites to appear .... In the end they came quietly, hung low in the murk almost directly overhead, then settled gently. The child knelt down in the rain, dismantled them, wrapped the tails and sticks in the sails and went away, singing. As he passed the shelter Celia called good night. He did not hear her, he was singing.

Her last sight of Murphy exerts a comparable tug: he 'holding the coat in against his waist before and behind, as though turned to stone in the middle of a hornpipe', she assailed many times thereafter by a last glimpse of his hand clutching a spike of railing, 'the fingers loosening and tightening, higher than the dark head'. Fingers and a dark head to be cherished in memory, such is the notation of human yearning. A grotesque, 'as though turned to stone in the middle of a hornpipe', such is the notation of the comic vision. If the comic vision is denied to Celia, that fact is to her advantage, strangely. Increasingly she resembles the pure sound of a flute intermixed with the clangour of some *Ballet mécanique*: a lyric theme to establish that the comic vision pervasive in the book does not bespeak authorial insensibility.

We have Neary, Wylie, Cooper, Miss Counihan, then, the grotesques, though normal to the daylight eye; we have Murphy, grotesque to the eye but comprehensible to the mind because of his wish to absent himself from daylight and its systems; and Celia, wistful denizen of a world of pure loss: who loves Murphy, inexplicably; who is deserted by him, logically; and measures the logic of that desertion by her pain.

The logic of desertion arises from the fact that Murphy finds his promised land elsewhere. He finds it in the madhouse. The patients, 'cut off ... from the rudimentary blessings of the layman's reality', enjoy, he supposes, just that suspension from the machine he has always craved. He thinks of them 'not as banished from a system of benefits but as escaped from a colossal fiasco', a fiasco such as the Counihans inhabit and the Nearys, such as the Celia who has nagged him to find work inhabits. He is soothed by 'the absolute impassiveness of the higher schizoids, in the face of the most pitiless therapeutic bombardment', and the padded cells seem to him 'indoor bowers of bliss'. He moves his rocking-chair into a garret, commandeers a gas fire, and settles into a ritual of fellowship with the patients, including chess with one of them, and of rocking. The world of linkages and causes pursues him, however, even here, in that the gas for his fire must be turned on in the watercloset downstairs. It is controlled there by a ring on a chain, similar to the ring and chain supplied by the plumbers for a different purpose. One day an anonymous hand will mistake the one chain for the other, and flush the rocking Murphy out of life. That hand works no more at random, we are to suppose, than the hand of God.

On his last night he plays a chess game, the forty-three moves of which the reader is advised to follow on a board. It enacts, as in a ballet, Murphy's fascination with the rituals of the 'higher schizoids', and his imperfect grasp of their satisfactions. His opponent, Mr Endon, whose name is the Greek word for 'within', has no interest whatever in the mock-warfare of the board. He is working out with his black pieces a pretty little rite of symmetry, which involves deploying his pieces and then returning them to their original state, in majestic indifference to capture, to threat of being captured, indeed to any manoeuvre of White's at all. White is irrelevant to Mr Endon; White's moves have this one significance for him only, that they indicate his own turn to move again. A less sensitive opponent than Murphy would run wild among these black pieces like a ravening wolf, with deplorable results for Mr Endon's equanimity (how could he play out his pattern if pieces got lost?). An opponent more fully attuned to Mr Endon's state would attempt a symmetrical ritual likewise, in utter indifference to Mr Endon. Murphy neither disturbs Mr Endon's game nor succeeds in aping its beauty, despite a hesitant mirroring, several times, of moves Mr Endon made two moves before. The game ends with Mr Endon's black pieces all compacted nearly as initially, a ballet of eerie and intricate beauty accomplished, only a King and two pawns displaced, while Murphy's pieces are scattered about the board in utter chaos, nearly the 'superfine chaos' of the gas that will shortly invade his lungs. It is as bizarre a climax as has been conceived for a novel.

There remains only the reunion of all parties (in the madhouse mortuary); the reading of Murphy's finely cadenced Will; Cooper's failure to execute its provisions; and Celia's solitude, alone with her uncle and his kite. She is back 'on the streets', satisfying the demands of numerous bodies. Her mind is permanently elsewhere, her yearning permanently unappeasable. She looks to the sky for 'that unction of soft sunless light on her eyes that was all she remembered of Ireland'. The book swells to a lyric finale. In Beckett's world there will be sad indomitable women again, notably Maddy Rooney in *All That Fall* and Winnie in *Happy Days*, women who have undergone a longer lifetime's damage, like Celias grown old; but not another Celia.

Clearly the author of *Murphy* had insufficient faith in 'the novel' to return to that form with any ambition of improving his management of it. Murphy's self-binding shifts the book out of the universe of verisimilitude, Murphy's chess game shifts an important part of its denouement out of the universe of language, and as for the third universe of fiction, the universe of causality, whatever in *Murphy* dwells within that universe is made fun of. These are all calculations, not mistakes. If it is possible to regard Celia as a mistake, diminishing as she does the coherent comic vision with pathos strayed as if from a different order of fiction, it is also possible to regard her as a hostage, gladly given, to ensure that the comic vision will be seen for what it is, an act of judgment, not a lack of competence. So a careful pastel might establish that cartoon figures within the same composition are stylizations and not scribbles.

But clearly the writer's real interest is Murphy. Clearly, too, the disruption of a classic form which from local evidence we deem that the author could have managed quite well had he wanted to stemmed not from a restless desire for formal play but from an awareness that a Murphy, given to the inner world, will baffle fiction's normal procedures. Retreating to his mind, he withdraws from the arena of agents and actions. Two time-honoured devices for presenting the reclusive hero were both of them unsuitable: the soliloquy, the interior monologue. The soliloquy is an act of spurning what Murphy cares about too little to spurn: he is no prose Childe Harold. The interior monologue depends for its substance on noting just such external particulars as Murphy is withdrawing from. It is a record of low-level perception, not an act of disengagement.

Beckett's next step, as though not sure what else to do, was to translate *Murphy* into French, a not inconsiderable feat, and then put the translation away in a drawer. What he might have done after that, pursuing some abstract logic of development, there is no telling; for in 1940 France was occupied, and it was no longer possible for him, even in fun, even as a rigorous academic joke, to suppose that peace lay in Murphy's little world. Murphy in the dark of his mind's third, highest state, amid 'nothing but commotion and the pure forms of commotion . . . not free, but a mote in the dark of absolute freedom', receded into the 1930s, a dream, and into the author's youth. His successors, Watt, Molloy, Moran, Malone, share his unassimilability but not his bliss. As much as they spurn the great world, it invades them, and their desperation lies in the effort to comprehend it, word it, narrate it.

NOTE ON THE CHESS GAME

Murphy (White) plays better than one may at first suppose, at least by this game's special definition of 'better'. After his initial, normal move he recognizes Black's weakness—Black's first move is simply unplayable—and, one gathers in an exploratory way, begins to imitate Black. But because of his first move he can't imitate Black successfully. Adding to his frustration is a growing sense that the game will never end. He tries desperately to give away pieces, but Black ignores them; he advances his King in the hope of being mated, and Black, without paying attention, avoids mating him; for one wild moment he threatens mate, but Black, without noticing, parries the threat, and after that White has no desire to win.

From the first he tries to please Black, to play Black's game, and at certain points—for instance move 23—we see how entangled he has become, how hard it is to imitate the imperturbable Black. Occasionally he anticipates Black's non-chessic moves, imitating them beforehand. He understands the non-logic, as though manifesting initiation into the norms of the oblivion he soon will undergo.[6]

5 Watt

Beckett in Paris at the beginning of the war was a neutral Irishman with arms folded. But Nazi harrassment of his Jewish friends, and Nazi shooting of hostages, conquered his detachment and led to anger, then to action. By the first winter of the Occupation he was collating, editing and typing scraps of information about troop movements for a far-flung Resistance group that survived nearly two years before a captured man betrayed it under torture. (Everyone who hears of such a thing must wonder what he would have done himself; and increasingly, in Beckett's later work, communication becomes something *extorted*.) Many of the group, at one time or another, would have waited at some French crossroads for some Godot; Beckett himself, even, may have been somebody's Godot, unable to come today but surely tomorrow. Others, who fell into the Gestapo's hands, would have been in the position of many of his protagonists, repeatedly commanded to talk without knowing what it was they were expected to say. Normally one knew one's immediate contacts, left and right in the chain; one knew, so far as it could be managed, nothing else. The 'Think, pig' which Pozzo addresses to Lucky is a first effort to come to terms with this intolerable possibility, that people might be forced to unwilling speech; it is more like an oral examination, however, than an inquisition, and Lucky's discourse is appropriately academic. It was only after twenty years, in 1963, that he used the stark situation directly, in the play called (grimly) *Play* in which a man and two women rehearse and rehearse their unsatisfactory testimony at the whim of an inquisitorial spotlight. This is perhaps a glimpse, tentative and to be used with caution, into the psychology of his creative process: a sense of having been solicited by realities so nearly unbearable that art can only come to terms with them slowly, through substitutions, at many tentative removes, until when the actuality is approximated it has been so purified of circumstance we do not recognize it for what it is. The central metaphor of *Play*, the immobilized speakers accosted by the light, has drawn down contempt for its formulaic despairingness, or its alleged want of meaning, from a generation of journalists who know perfectly well about the SS.

When the Resistance group was betrayed the Gestapo pounced. Beckett and Suzanne, forewarned, had left their apartment minutes earlier. With forged papers, two months later, they made their dangerous way through the occupied zone to the unoccupied, and at last to a village called Rousillon where 'for two and a half years Beckett's life and Suzanne's depended literally on his ability to pass himself off as a French peasant, and to earn enough money by the sweat of his brow to pay for their food.' After one potato harvest he got permission to glean in the field; 'under conditions prevailing in those days, finding a potato in the sea of mud was like finding a gold nugget.' (Food, and crawling through mud, still occupied the imagination of the author of *How It Is* after two decades). And he chopped wood for a man named Aude in return for the weekly hospitality of a meal. And, in the evenings, in exercise books, he wrote *Watt*, about a man moved into a dim unintelligible world where he is a servant.

But this is too neat. *Watt* is no more a self-portrait than was *Murphy*, and Watt's is not an Occupation story. If the Occupation and attendant flight and derangement and intellectual darkness impressed themselves on *Watt* (and on all Beckett's subsequent work), they did so by providing categories, not contents: occasions for analysis of the grim business of survival amidst uncertainties, ambiguities. Ambiguity, uncertainty, these are ever afterward the notes of his great world, and no Beckett protagonist ever again finds peace, such a peace as (albeit intermittently, imperfectly) Murphy found, closing his eyes, abandoning his body, rocking, rocking, secured by scarves, the mystic seven.

The artist is never not engaged with his own development, with discovering and pursuing its internal logic, whatever may be happening in the great world. Those happenings give him nutriment, or give him cues, and we can often identify their impress. But we can also trace an evolutionary logic from which it seems that the development we discern was the only development possible, that it would have gone forward anyway whatever the course of personal accident or public event. 'The man of genius', says Joyce, 'makes no mistakes; his errors are volitional and are the portals of discovery.' (It was Beckett's 'error', his mother and brothers may have supposed, not to have stayed where he was in Ireland when the Wehrmacht moved across the Polish frontier; but he made his way back to France just in time to be trapped there.) And, wrote Joyce, 'Every life is many days, day after day. We walk through ourselves, meeting robbers, ghosts, giants, old men, young men, wives, widows, brothers-in-love. But always meeting ourselves.' It was in some such sense that Beckett's imagination encountered Watt.

Watt looks as queer as Murphy. ('Mr Hackett was not sure that it was not a parcel, a carpet for example, or a roll of tarpaulin, wrapped up in dark paper and tied about the middle with a cord.') 'Like a sewer-pipe, said Mrs Nixon. Where are his arms?' The people to whom he looks as queer as this themselves talk queerly, somewhat as did Wylie and Neary; but whereas Wylie's and Neary's queer talk was addressed to such recondite matters as the fate of Hippasos the Akousmatic,[7] and thus enwrapped itself by right in pedantic precision, the people of the great world in the first part of *Watt* always manage to sound, on the most banal of topics, as though their discourse were being translated from some tongue of bizarre civility:

These north-western skies are really extraordinary, said Goff, are they not.

So voluptuous, said Tetty. You think it is all over and then pop!
up they flare, with augmented radiance.

Such discourse, for all its ease, moves amid submarine grotesqueries, so we are not surprised to find that minds governed
by its canons cannot assimilate Watt. Not that minds governed
by your canons or mine have better success. When Watt, as
we learn, with one foot bare, seven years ago borrowed five
shillings 'to buy himself a boot', Mr Hackett's objection has
force, that 'One does not buy a boot'; when we learn some
two hundred pages later that he required but one boot because
he had just found a shoe on the strand, we are somewhat
enlightened, and when the availability of one boot is accounted
for we are enlightened still more (he had bought it for eight
pence 'from a one-legged man who, having lost his leg, and
a fortiori his foot, in an accident, was happy to realize, on his
discharge from hospital, for such a sum, his unique remaining
marketable asset'). But as tokens of a way of life these facts
are puzzling, and it is still more puzzling, even if coincidental,
that after seven years Watt has in his pockets exactly the change
that would have remained after that transaction, four shillings
and fourpence, *i.e.* five shillings less eightpence. Are we to
suppose that he has spent not another penny in all those years?
But by the time these data are all in our possession it has been
irresistably borne upon us that there is only one profitable
way to think of Watt, if profitable is the word. He is a character
in a fiction, determined by such symmetries as may amuse
the author, who may also choose to infect his text with local
uncertainties ('Watt had a poor healing skin, and perhaps
his blood was deficient in ? ') and may also choose to bring
Watt a long journey to 'Mr Knott's House' without venturing
any explanation of why Watt is going there.
    Pervasive as ozone, uncertainty invests the pores and inter-
stices of the narrative. Who Mr Knott may be we do not discover, which is to say that we can neither fit him into a
recognizable socio-economic system, nor visualize him, nor
lay hold of his repertory of mannerisms: this despite the fact

that numerous habits and customs of his are reported, his
habit for instance of changing his position each night on his
circular bed so as to execute a revolution once in a year,[8] or
his addiction to 'solitary dactylic ejaculations of extraordinary
vigour, accompanied by spasms of the members. The chief
of these were: Exelmans! Cavendish! Habbakuk! Ecchymose!'
Nor do we discover why Watt has entered his service, though
we do discover that Watt's arrival is the cue for his predecessor
to leave. There are always two servants, it seems, and when
a new one arrives the junior is promoted and the senior departs.
Later Arthur arrives and Watt is promoted; still later Micks
arrives, and Watt departs. No rationale for these arrangements
is offered. There is a pattern of tall and knock-kneed servants,
among whom Vincent, Walter, Watt, and small fat bowlegged
servants, among whom Arsene, Erskine, Arthur, but this pattern
does not quite enjoin the strict alternation of types that would
ensure there being always on the premises a Laurel type and
a Hardy type. Thus for instance Arsene and Erskine were
both present at once, and both fat, and Vincent and Walter
both present at once, and both thin. This is a minor example
of an important principle, that the book repeatedly drives us
to search after patterns, which turn out to be less neat than we
should like. There has been, and this is all we can tell, an
indefinitely long series of servants, always two present at once,
and always belonging, one or both at a time, to one of two
physical types—this exposition begins to sound like a page
out of *Watt*, which is unsurprising, since the style of *Watt* is
the most efficient that can be discovered for expounding the
kind of material *Watt* contains. The analyst whose stock-in-
trade is his skill at putting his author's matter before his reader
in pithier or less redundant language will find no purchase
here.

We may notice two things in particular about the style of
Watt, that it is tirelessly explicit, and that it eschews the semi-
colon. ('How hideous is the semi-colon,' the author comments,
on a rare page to which this punctuation mark is admitted.)
This means that the habit of stopping for more judicious

rephrasing, or the habit of joining one clause to another in temporal or causal subordination, are both foreign to its texture.[9] Instead sentences trail off among alternatives ('Or we saw a big black bird perched in the void, perhaps croaking, or preening its feathers'), or else entertain sets of equipotent possibilities ('Lower voices, voices more rapid, have been heard, will be heard, than Watt's voice, no doubt'), or dangle before us a whole Calderesque mobile of elements conducing toward explicitness, the explicitness that is the book's hallmark. 'For reasons that remain obscure Watt was, for a time, greatly interested, and even fascinated, by this matter of the dog, the dog brought into the world, and maintained there, at considerable expense, for the sole purpose of eating Mr Knott's food, on those days on which Mr Knott was not pleased to eat it himself, and he attached to this matter an importance, and even a significance, that seem hardly warranted.' 'For reasons that remain obscure', this sentence begins, and then sees to it that nothing but those reasons shall remain touched by the least obscurity. And the entire book is in this way a raid of syntax upon chaos, establishing what syntax can establish, and rhythm, and pattern, and precision of naming, amid a pervasive incompetence, a climate of hearsay, and a tendency of the data to shift.

Thus the reader, coping with the book, finds his position to be not unlike that of the writer, writing it, and Watt, experiencing it. Murphy, however he may have resembled his creator, was always unlike the reader, always, in his act of rejecting the great world, rejecting also the landmarks that are familiar to literate lookers-on. So we found him simply strange. But in this book, such is its insidious advance upon its predecessor, the reader tends to finds that he is becoming Watt. The question of the dogs and the food, just broached, engages the reader as it engaged Watt, there being nothing else to be engaged by, and the terms of the question being so enigmatically simple. 'But once Watt had grasped, in its complexity, the mechanism of this arrangement, how the food came to be left, and the dog to be available, and the two to be united, then it interested him no more, and he enjoyed a comparative peace of mind, in this connexion.' We share, to some extent, that peace of mind. 'Not that for a moment Watt supposed that he had penetrated the forces at play, in this particular instance, or even perceived the forms that they upheaved, or obtained the least useful information concerning himself, or Mr Knott, for he did not.' We share that estimate of the subject's elusiveness, and its uselessness. 'But he had turned, little by little, a disturbance into words, he had made a pillow of old words, for his head.' We share that sense too, in a way, as participating savourers of those words, and the author surely has shared it, and more deeply, and this strange symbiosis of writer, character and reader is the great advance over *Murphy* that this book registers.

The book's four-part symmetry is the first symmetry of many. Part one, Watt steps out of the great world into the not-world of Knott. Two, Watt's term as a junior servant, on the ground floor. Three, Watt's term as senior servant, on the first floor, in direct attendance upon Mr Knott. Four, Watt departs, and returns to the station. In the third part we learn, moreover, that Watt and the writer, named Sam, spent time together in an institution of some sort, its nature unspecified. Sam, therefore, is not the omniscient author, for his information has all come from Watt, in fits and starts and uncertainties, entoiled with the increasing peculiarities—carefully specified— of Watt's communication. Thus Sam can indulge the gesture of reporting that some trivial fact is 'not known', quite as though historical research were in question. And yet Sam knows more, much more, than Watt could have told him, for instance the conversations on the opening and closing pages, the voices of the great world, dismissing Watt. It is useless to apply logic to this consideration, as useless as it has been to apply it elsewhere in the book, where all coherence has been provisional.

Each of the two middle parts contains one detachable set-piece: the episode of the Lynch family, the academic episode of Louit. The Lynch family's very warrant for existence in the book is that Watt found it necessary to dwell on them, as he retraced the possible steps by which, long ago, the problem of the dogs had been solved. Outside Watt's thought, though, the extent of their existence is, to say the least, dubious. Reason entails a dog's custodian; experience seems to confirm two of them, twin dwarfs. But whereas by Occam's Razor beings are not to be postulated beyond necessity, the dogs' custodians, once postulated, commence to swarm and pullulate and acquire genealogies, diseases, obsessions, disappointments, triumphs. We may be meant to wonder whether God's experience has been like Watt's, his creation escaping as if of its own accord from the scope of his severe purposes. Certainly theologians have had such experiences, having postulated angels with scriptural warrant, and then found themselves equipping battalions and hierarchies of angels with names, specialties, characters, even with a history of heavenly warfare.

This is a good example, we may note in passing, of one of the sources of the book's fascination, its passage through so many familiar paradigms. The temptation to allegorize it is consequently strong. Watt exemplifies, for instance, the Questor motif, entering a dark forest. Though no allegory will fit, we are conscious of the appeal of many allegories. The effort to resist them is like the effort to keep two strong magnets a half-inch apart with our fingers when the lines of invisible force strain toward union.

The Lynch family, to pursue that motif a little further, has an engaging obsession. There are twenty-eight of them at first count, and they long for the day when their combined ages will total one thousand years. We are given their ages, which we may find total 978 years; we are told that the total is 980 years; we are told moreover that 'the figures given here are incorrect', and 'the consequent calculations . . . therefore doubly erroneous'. We are told of Kate, age twenty-one, that she was 'a fine girl but a bleeder', and also told, in the book's most magisterial footnote, that haemophilia is exclusively a male disorder, 'but not in this work'. It may be that the sum of the figures given, 85, 65, 64, . . . 4, 3, is not 978 'in this work' either. That would explain much, and we may remember non-Euclidean geometry, and the humbler anecdote, in part one, of the man who announced quite gratuitously and at great inconvenience that it was 5.17 just when Big Ben struck 6.00, and also the opinion, voiced by Arsene in that connection, that such is 'the type of all information whatsoever, be it voluntary or solicited'.

The Lynches, moreover, are riddled with disease, in fact with specified diseases, and their number includes a cousin Sam 'whose amorous disposition was notorious', and who moves about on his adulterous errands in a self-propelling invalid's chair; for 'paralysed as he was, from the waist up, and from the knees down, he had no purpose, interest or joy in life other than this, to set out after a good dinner of meat and vegetables in his wheel-chair and stay out committing adultery until it was time to go home to his supper, after which he was at his wife's disposal'. Only fictional characters are so potent, and this Sam is doubly fictional, being a figment of Watt's whose lucubrations are being reported to us by a different Sam, who together with Watt was conceived, in evenings after the hoeing of potatoes, by yet a third Sam, Sam Beckett.

As for the Louit episode, framed by encomiums to a potent aphrodisiac named Bando (French *bander*, to be aroused; not in genteel dictionaries), its foci are likewise numerical, Louit's dissertation being on *The Mathematical Intuitions of the Visicelts* and the principal episode being his production, before a Grants Committee, of an alleged Visicelt who can extract cube roots in his head. As elsewhere in *Watt*, the simplest communication bogs down in procedural elaboration, and while the new junior servant, Arthur, who tells the story, does so in order to transport his imagination 'far from Mr Knott's premises, of which, of the mysteries of which, of the fixity of which, Arthur had sometimes more than he could bear', yet it is into the same order of mystery that the story leads him, and when he breaks the story off it is because his imagination has been absent an unbearable time from Mr Knott's house, its mysteries, its fixity. The operative word would seem to be *fixity*. Mystery is not peculiar to Mr Knott's house, mystery is everywhere. Sand runs out of every being at every seam. But in Mr Knott's house the mysteries are at least circumscribed.

These mysteries have to do with the incapacity of language, and hence of thought which operates (in this work) through language alone, to locate with finality any datum, or define with assurance any relation. One long quotation will make this point clear.

Watt was surprised to find the back door, so lately locked, now open. Two explanations of this occurred to him. The first was this, that his science of the locked door, so seldom at fault, had been so on this occasion, and that the back door, when he had found it locked, had not been locked, but open. And the second was this, that the back door, when he had found it locked, had in effect been locked, but had subsequently been opened, from within, or without, by some person, while he Watt had been employed in going, to and fro, from the back door to the front door, and from the front door to the back door.

Of these two explanations Watt thought he preferred the latter, as being more beautiful. For if someone had opened the back door, from within, or without, would not he Watt have seen a light, or heard a sound? Or had the door been unlocked, from within, in the dark, by some person perfectly familiar with the premises, and wearing carpet slippers, or his stockinged feet? Or, from without, by some person so skilful on his legs, that his footfalls made no sound? Or had a sound been made, or a light shown, and Watt not heard the one nor seen the other?

The result of this was that Watt never knew how he got into Mr Knott's house. . . .

This is characteristic of the narrative movement in *Watt*. So many trivia are entoiled in such uncertainty that the author cannot make with any confidence the simplest narrative gesture. And being scrupulous, he itemizes the possibilities: so much can mind do, and language do. And sentences about what did not happen are if anything more precise than sentences about what did, since in the ideal world of logic and language it may be specified with utter certainty that if a sound is made, and detected, it will be heard, and if a light is made, and detected, it will be seen, since no other verbs are admissible. But sentences that attempt to state what did happen are likely to unravel.

The book chokes, therefore, slowly, on its own internal elaborations, redeemed however—this is nicely calculated—by the ceremony, the rhythm, in short the great formal beauty of all those gentle scrupulous sentences. Provisionality, from being a point of epistemology, becomes almost a point of etiquette, as though to affirm anything at all—to affirm that Watt passed through a door—would be a discourtesy to the reader, a bullying. Sam, the narrator of *Watt*, though we know him only by the manners of his prose, is excellent company, agreeable, unintimidating. *Watt* is like a rope of sand, dissolving before our eyes as it is narrated, but Sam is never ruffled, never ruffled.

6 Mercier et Camier

It is convenient to postulate, without being wholly sure, that *Mercier et Camier* was Beckett's first post-war work, despite hints that he had already begun *Molloy* when he wrote it. He was unconvinced by it, described it as 'jettisoned', but nevertheless allowed acquaintances to read a typescript of which they would not have suspected the existence but for his mention of it, permitted bits to be quoted and translated, resisted all overtures toward publication, finally weakened after more than twenty years ('I'll weaken some day,' he had said five years previously), and as this is written, is working sporadically on an English version. That is the way a man treats a 'transitional' work, the first step toward the idiosyncratic vertigo of his most famous novels, and apparently his first extended writing in French.

The change of language deserves a moment's attention. In 1937-9, after *Murphy*, before *Watt*, just after finally settling in Paris, Beckett had written a dozen French poems, dying as it were into an alien tongue, the one by which he had chosen to be surrounded thenceforward. To write in a language one has learned in classrooms is to be committed to vigilance, deliberation: to be aware of grammar, of syntax, above all of idiom, as it is difficult to be in a language one cannot remember not having spoken. This detachment, one may speculate, will remain no matter how habitual the second language becomes.

Detachment, deliberation, awareness, these have been for more than a century the notes of modernity. To write in a

foreign language is the extreme term of a process of which
another form is exemplified by Americans and Irishmen assuming (like Eliot) or resisting (like Pound) the idiom of a literary
capital, and yet another form by Flaubert or Joyce taking
pains so far as possible, with the aid of dictionaries and second
thoughts, to approach the native idiom as if it were a foreign
language. Between the 'style' which is but a gracefulness in
doing the natural thing, and the 'style' toward the achievement of which Flaubert tormented himself at the rate of a
few sentences a day, the difference is that the former can become reasonably facile (with a little practice one can 'do'
Pater's style; Yeats did, habitually), whereas the latter can
never be a role, can only be a wrestle, clause by clause, syllable
perhaps by syllable, with the things no native speaker gives
a thought to. In pre-modern style, before the Flaubertian
Revolution, the 'ordinary' sentences of an utterance were
linguistic environment, simply there, unattended to. Occasional
jewels-five-words-long conferred distinction. But it was just
the 'environmental' part of language that Flaubert raised to
visibility. The ordinary idioms, the little banalities, were as
efficacious, he saw, in shaping his characters' minds as the other
environmental ordinarinesses on which he bestowed such attention: chairs, wall-hangings, hats, garden walls with espaliered
apricots.

   In *Watt* Beckett devoted pages of close attention to the look
of order declarative sentences impart, however slight their
content, simply by being sentences, therefore orderly: offering
to excise for our attention 'subjects' and 'objects', and encap-
sulate seamless intricacies of process as 'verbs'. But Watt
had trouble framing a sentence about a pot, because he had
trouble with the very word 'pot'. What might it betoken,
Watt wondered, to excise from the flux of appearance this
stability, to imitate it and nail it into place with this monosyllable, to 'say pot, pot, and be comforted'? And this order
of attention to the simplest assumptions of language is easier
for the writer, and seems less odd to the reader, when the writer
is subjected to the discipline of a language of which he learned

grammar faster than vocabulary, where he has the habit of paying attention to everything, and in which the most banal idioms—'*Comment vous portez-vous?*'—were once, in some classroom, objects of distinct attention. There are passages in *Waiting for Godot* and *Endgame* that sound, particularly in the French original, like classroom drill.

And this separating of attention from habit is particularly to be expected when the foreign language is French, where the 'normal' vocabulary is distinguishable from the erudite or the exotic to a degree impossible in English, and where the conventions of syntax and word-order are relatively rigorous. (To write English well, said Eliot, you must approach it with *animosity*.) The strangely pedantic precision of so many paragraphs in *Watt* corresponds to a texture normal in French prose. Despite the formal correctness of every sentence, and in part even because of that correctness, *Watt* is already strange English. It has even the air, at times, of relying on French for its idioms; we read of a tramcar's 'facultative' Stop, and find 'in effect' used as though it were 'en effet'. To pursue this line of development without the texture growing even stranger—misleadingly strange—it was convenient for Beckett to adopt a French base. His English fictions, subsequent to *Watt*, are arrived at by translation from a French original. The French texts, moreover, far from serving as intermediate drafts, are accorded autonomous status and published in France, normally before the work of making the English version has even begun. So every Beckett work has a dual aspect and a dual life, it being impossible that the nuances of the two versions should accord. How the French originals strike French readers an alien cannot guess—beyond the fact that critics seem not to take exception to details of usage—but indisputably the English versions arrived at by this process constitute something new in English prose.

In *Mercier et Camier* certain initial precisions, certain initial formalities of idiom, were inherent in the fictional enterprise, to counterpoise the book's way of unravelling. And thinking in French, Beckett was enabled to develop his theme of circumambient aimlessness without being forced, as he had been in *Watt*, to devise a countervailing prose pedantic to the point of ludicrousness.

'*Le voyage de Mercier et Camier*,' runs the first sentence, '*je peux le raconter si je veux, car j'étais avec eux tout le temps.*' Translation word for word gives: 'The journey of Mercier and Camier, I can tell about it if I wish, for I was with them all the time.'

But the inverted word-order is unnatural in English, so: 'If I want to I can tell you all about the journey . . . '. Condition first: wrong, coy. 'I can tell you about the journey, if I want to . . . '. Narrator first: wrong, he is unimportant. The point of 'I was with them, all the time' (with perhaps, for English, a nuance imparted by a comma) is the sly point that I invented them, and made up their journey, every step of which, so far as steps are specified, they took with my deliberate cooperation. This point is blurred perhaps beyond retrieval if we are made aware in the first word of this 'I' who ought to be hiding his smile deep below the page.

All of which is but to say that the book is intimately shaped by French idiom, only to be translated by an unobtrusive tour de force of rethinking, phrase after phrase. Beckett's version of the first sentence runs: 'The journey of Mercier and Camier is one I can tell, if I wish, for I was with them all the time.'

The journey, then: an aimless journey, a theme to be greatly amplified in *Molloy*. Where they are going, why they are travelling, is utterly obscure. If it is obscure to them, they do not say so, anyhow not at first; and we are in the presence of that odd interaction between creator and creatures that in *Molloy* and *Malone Dies* will be intensified by the conventions of first-person narrative.

Perhaps the point of the journey is not obscure at all, perhaps the author has simply neglected to disclose it, or perhaps, since he is a novelist, he has reasons for deferring this disclosure until later. But the odd effect is that until we are made aware, Mercier and Camier are not made aware either. So we have them busying themselves with details of transport and man-

oeuvres of rendezvous quite as if they had no choice (they have
not; they are 'characters') and did not think to ask (they do
not, if the author does not make them).

   Their rendezvous is settled; Camier arrives first; Mercier
has not arrived; Camier goes for a walk. (No, that is not right;
it was Mercier who arrived first, and did not see Camier, and
went for a walk before Camier arrived.) And now Mercier
arrives in Camier's absence, and sees no one, and goes for
a walk . . . quite in the traditions of stage farce; and the narrator takes pains to draw up a timetable of arrivals and de-
partures:

	Arr.	Dep.	Arr.	Dep.	Arr.	Dep.	Arr.
Mercier	9.05	9.10	9.25	9.30	9.40	9.45	9.50
Camier	9.15	9.20	9.35	9.40	9.50		

Having furnished this he remarks, '*Que cela pue l'artifice*':
'How that reeks of artifice.'

   So the work proceeds. Chapter 1, their preparations and
rendezvous; Chapter 2, still in the city; whereupon we turn
a page and confront Chapter 3: 'Résumé of the preceding
chapters.' It is just that, a checklist of topics:

Setting forth.
Difficult meeting of Mercier and Camier.
Saint-Ruth Square.
The purple beech.
The rain.
The shelter.
The dogs.
Camier's depression.
The guard.
The bicycle.
Dispute with the guard. . . . *etc.*

What does this mean? It means, once more, that this is artifice, all this narrative. It means, perhaps, since novels if they
are Significant Works exist in classrooms more than they exist

anywhere else, that we may be preparing ourselves to be examined on it, and may welcome a summary to spare us the trouble of making our own. It means that the narrator, despite the look of aimlessness which implies low-pressure improvisation, has reread what he has written, and let it stand; moreover that its drift can be pegged and mensurated by a series of headings. And it means that the narrator is engaged in examination of his narrative, which means examination of his fantasies, which means self-examination: a very clipped and very austere self-examination, to be sure, one affirming no conclusions, no regrets, no satisfactions, but nevertheless a scrupulous backward look. Some of the material has been salacious, some of it perverse; yet having gone over it at least twice he has suppressed none of it, though we cannot affirm that he has seen, like God in Genesis, that it is good. We can say that he has seen it, with whatever smothering of conscience, whatever show of indifference. There has even been one quite outrageous happening:

A terrible screech of brakes rent the air, followed by a scream and a resounding crash. Mercier and Camier made a rush (after a moment's hesitation) for the open street and were rewarded by the vision, soon hidden by a concourse of sightseers, of a big fat woman, apparently well on in life, writhing feebly on the ground. The disorder of her dress revealed an amazing mass of billowing underclothes, originally white in colour. Her blood, streaming from one or more wounds, had already reached the gutter.
    Ah, said Mercier, that's what I needed, I feel a new man.
    He was in fact transfigured.
    Let that be a lesson to us, said Camier.
    Meaning? said Mercier.
    Never to despair, said Camier, or lose our faith in life.

Even this the author has not thought better of, entering it in his summary as 'The accident', and accepting, maybe, the disorder of sensibility from which it arose when he wrote it down.

Or being oblivious to that disorder; for this is one of Beckett's imagined narrators, a different one altogether from the patient engaging Sam who accepts responsibility for *Watt*. This narrator goes in for perversely poetical landscapes:

Where are our feet trying to take us? said Camier.
In my opinion, said Mercier, we are heading for the canal.
Already? said Camier.
Perhaps it will give us pleasure, said Mercier, to take the towpath and follow it till boredom doth ensue. Before us, beckoning us on, without our having to lift up our eyes, the dying colours we love so well.
Speak for yourself, said Camier.
The water too, said Mercier, will linger livid, which is not to be despised either. And then, who knows, the fancy may take us to throw ourselves in.
The little bridges slip by, said Camier, ever fewer and farther between. We pore over the locks, trying to understand. From the barges made fast to the bank waft the watermen's voices, to wish us good-evening. Their day is done, they smoke a last pipe before turning in.

This set-piece appears in the Résumé as 'Evocation of the canal'; only that, though feeling has come uncongealed during the composing of it. A dozen years later Beckett conceived Krapp, playing over the tape he recorded three decades earlier and lingering on a segment which at the time he had entered in his ledger only as 'Farewell to Love'. The segments which had celebrated great insight leave him impatient now. These Résumés are a first glimpse of Krapp's ledger; the narrator of *Mercier et Camier* is a proto-Krapp. Between this novel of 1946 and the 1958 play we shall traverse novels in which the man writing and the thing written occupy a simultaneous foreground, the writing itself in part an indulgence, in part a self-examination.

The Résumé, the writer keeping score, is the first salient originality of *Mercier et Camier*. Its second originality is to be found in dialogues of stylized inanity, later to serve as the substantive texture of *Godot*. They have decided not to throw away an umbrella which is more like a parasol:

Very well, said Camier, but the question is not only do we throw it away, the question is also are we to put it up.

But is it not in part with a view to putting it up, said Mercier, that we refrain from throwing it away?

True, said Camier, but are we to put it up here and now or wait till the weather is more marked?

Mercier scrutinized the inscrutable sky.

Go and take a look, he said, and tell me what you think.

Camier went out into the street. He even pushed on to the corner, so that Mercier lost sight of him. On his return he said:

It could be lightening from below. Shall I go on the roof?

Mercier concentrated. Finally he said, impulsively:

Put it up and come what may.

But Camier could not put it up.

Give it here, said Mercier.

But Mercier had no better success. He raised it high above his head, but controlled himself in time. Proverb.

What have we done to God? He said.

Denied him, said Camier.

Don't tell me he's all that uncharitable, said Mercier.

'How lamentable all this is', remarks the dejected author; much as, having devised a childhood for the man in his story, the dying Malone will adjoin, 'What tedium', and much as Didi and Gogo in *Godot* will comment on just the emptiness of which the play's audience is growing conscious.

And the third innovation of *Mercier et Camier* is this, that the book very artfully runs down. It is not abandoned, for the final chapter, 12, is as usual the Résumé of the two previous chapters, 10 and 11. But clearly the narrative has ended, clearly there is no more to be done, nor to be said; clearly the journey has yielded no such benefits, no such satisfactions, as it seemed to promise, nor are we even certain for that matter that all their moving about has constituted the journey they envisaged. Clearly the elegiac retrospect of the two:

Do you remember the parrot? said Mercier.

I remember the goat, said Camier.

The parrot, said Mercier, I have the feeling it's dead.

We didn't meet with many animals, said Camier.

is a bidding farewell to the enterprise, theirs and the author's, the enterprise which never found means of consummating itself: a salute to entropy: a firmly stated dissolution.

The next books are about dissolution, reduction. They are reduced, they dissolve, and that is their theme. Must a flourish of trumpets consummate a novel? Life has few trumpets to offer.

7 The Trilogy

MOLLOY

Molloy begins, 'I am in my mother's room.' That is clear enough.
'It's I who live there now.' Also clear. 'I don't know how I
got there.' Succinct. And so on: short sentences setting forth
the elements of his present state, in which he writes out a statement for which, delivered in installments, a man comes every
week. It's not clear who wants it, or why, nor why they (it
is 'they', a kind of tolerant Gestapo) are displeased with the
way he began it. 'Here's my beginning,' he tells us. 'Here it
is.' There ensues an unbroken unparagraphed narrative,
nothing but easy chronological flow, some hundred pages of
it. Its sentences are not stacatto but long and easy, elegiac,
and it transports us without effort into uncertainties like those
of the world of *Watt*. 'It is in the tranquillity of decomposition
that I remember the long confused emotion which was my life',
and confusion is certainly the norm of its simplest episodes,
suffused though they are by the ceremony of leavetaking, for
Molloy will not be thinking of them again.

This time, then once more I think, then perhaps a last time, then I
think it'll be over, with that world too. Premonition of the last but
one but one. All grows dim. A little more and you'll grow blind. It's
in the head. It doesn't work any more, it says, I don't work any more.
You go dumb as well and sounds fade. The threshold scarcely crossed
that's how it is. It's the head. It must have had enough. So that you
say, I'll manage this time, then perhaps once more, then perhaps a
last time, then nothing more. . . .

'You go dumb as well and sounds fade': Vergil has no finer

cadence, no juxtaposition more sensitive to rhythms and vowels. There is more sustained emotion in the first half of *Molloy* than in anything else Beckett has written. 'Cows were chewing in enormous fields, lying and standing, in the evening silence.' How soothing are these cows, fixed in that amber cadence. How soothing, too, the elusively neutral landscape:

From there he must have seen it all, the plain, the sea, and then these selfsame hills that some call mountains, indigo in places in the evening light, their serried ranges crowding to the skyline, cloven with hidden valleys that the eye divines from sudden shifts of colour and then from other signs for which there are no words, nor even thoughts.

These are last looks, last thoughts; 'If you think of the forms and light of other days it is without regret,' and yet 'what magic in those dim things to which it will be time enough, when next they pass, to say goodbye.'

The emotion is sure, the events are as far from sureness as the events of *Watt*, though not from paucity of data (to be interrogated with fierce attention) but from uncertainty of memory (to be accepted, though often to be regretted). He recalls a kind of archetypal event, a meeting, observed by him from high up above that wide landscape: A and C meeting on an evening walk. They have left the town separately, one has turned back, they meet, exchange words inaudible at this great distance. Are they strangers or not? Then they go their ways, C onward, A back toward the town, and Molloy speculates first on the one who is going onward, '. . . innocent, greatly innocent, he had nothing to fear, though he went in fear, he had nothing to fear, there was nothing they could do to him, or very little. But he can't have known it. . . . Yes, he saw himself threatened, his body threatened, his reason threatened, and perhaps he was, perhaps they were, in spite of his innocence. What business has innocence here? What relation to the innumerable spirits of darkness?' That is perhaps an Occupation note, though it need not be; it applies quite as well to normal times. (The novel was written about 1947). And as to the one who is going back toward town, Molloy forgets by now if he is A or C, but speculates about him likewise, noting that he moved 'with a kind of loitering indolence which rightly or wrongly seemed to me expressive'. That sounds like a line from a detective novel, as indeed does the whole business of Molloy's surveillance of A and C, and his speculations about them. (Camier, incidentally, it emerges almost casually part way through *Mercier et Camier*, is a private detective.) But then Molloy starts to wonder if he is perhaps confusing several different occasions, 'And perhaps it was A one day at one place, then C another at another, then a third the rock and I, and so on for the other components, the cows, the sky, the sea, the mountains. I can't believe it. No, I will not lie, I can easily conceive it. No matter, no matter, let us go on.' And, a little later, 'A and C I never saw again.'

Not that we do not wonder whether one or another of the various people he does subsequently meet may be A or C, a meaningless question come to think of it, since whatever may be the case in real life, one character in a novel is identical with another character in a novel only if the author somehow, overtly or covertly, asserts that he is. But for the time being no author is in sight except Molloy. It is like this novel to play on our tendency to forget that we are reading a piece of writing, and also to remind us periodically of that fact. For the reader's uncertainties cannot surpass Molloy's, nor Molloy's the reader's. Molloy is Beckett's first venture in a new kind of character, what he once called in a letter 'the narrator/narrated'. It is a device he employs in all his subsequent fiction, bringing the ambient world into existence only so far as the man holding the pencil can remember it or understand it, so that no omniscient craftsman is holding anything back, and simultaneously bringing into existence the man with the pencil, who is struggling to create himself, so to speak, by recalling his own past or delineating his own present. As *Watt* was a step beyond *Murphy*, and *Mercier et Camier* a hesitant step beyond *Watt*, so this is a further step, into uncharted, foreordained terrain. The business of filling the air with uncertainty, the uncertainty fiction normally dissipates, need no longer be left to style,

style being now identical with the uncertain mental processes of a protagonist.

The outline of Molloy's story is deceptively simple. After seeing A and C out of sight, he resolves to go and see his mother. There is no reason for this resolve, moreover he hates her, but the purpose consumes him. He sets off on his bicycle. He falls foul of the police, also for no reason. This episode establishes the extent to which he and officialdom inhabit totally different worlds, so that neither has the faintest grasp of what the other is saying. He meets a woman named Mrs Lousse as a result of running over her dog, and is kept in her house for a while at her behest, it is unclear why. He leaves there on his crutches, abandoning the bicycle; loses interest in his mother and leaves town; is attracted by his mother again and attempts to find town again; and beset by steady physical disintegration (stiffening of his good leg, shortening of a leg, loss of toes, loss of strength, arthritis in wrists) he wanders, then crawls, then lies immobile in a ditch. He has heard a voice, which may be hallucinatory: 'Don't fret Molloy, we're coming.' He does not fret. He does not even wish. 'Molloy could stay, where he happened to be.'

Such an outline, it is clear, conveys little; the events are unimportant. What is important (a word to be used with diffidence) is the look of aimlessness itself, the degeneration, then, of purpose into crawling, the degeneration of body into physical wreckage, and the degeneration of the lyricism that observed A and C and their landscape into a savage and prickly distaste for all phenomena, not excluding self and not excluding language. For instance,

But I also said, Yet a little while, at the rate things are going, and I won't be able to move, but will have to stay, where I happen to be, unless someone comes and carries me. Oh I did not say it in such limpid language. And when I say I said, etc., all I mean is that I knew confusedly things were so, without knowing exactly what it was all about. And every time I say, I said this, or, I said that, or speak of a voice saying, far away inside me, Molloy, and then a fine phrase more or less clear and simple, or find myself compelled to attribute to others intelligible words, or hear my own voice uttering to others more or less articulate sounds, I am merely complying with the convention that demands you either lie or hold your peace.

The world grows slowly sour, grows infected, grows repellent. Nevertheless the mind will not be still, and working away amid phenomena it has no taste for, it achieves without laughing an ever blacker, ever wilder comedy.

And I even crawled on my back, plunging my crutches blindly behind me into the thickets, and with the black boughs for sky to my closing eyes. I was on my way to mother. And from time to time I said, Mother, to encourage me I suppose. I kept losing my hat, the lace had broken long ago, until in a fit of temper I banged it down on my skull with such violence that I couldn't get it off again. And if I had met any lady friends, if I had any lady friends, I would have been powerless to salute them correctly.

Imagine, in such a pass, thinking of saluting ladies correctly! Imagine, for that matter, being human: which is what *Molloy*, in its fashion, incites us to do.

At this point a new narrator takes up a new tale. 'My name is Moran, Jacques. That is the name I am known by. I am done for. My son too. All unsuspecting. He must think he's on the threshold of life, of real life. He's right there. His name is Jacques, like mine. This cannot lead to confusion.'

He is right in rejecting an identity of names as a source of confusion, but wrong if he supposes there will be no confusion, for into confusion, of Molloy's inimitable kind, Moran sinks: that is the substance of his narrative.

Molloy, on the second page of his narrative, had speculated whether he had a son. 'But I think not. He would be old now, nearly as old as myself . . . . It seems to me sometimes that I even knew my son, that I helped him. Then I tell myself it's impossible.' The fact that both narrators' names begin with Mo is the first similarity between them. The turning of the narrative toward a son is the second; and as Moran's tale proceeds the similarities multiply. They are even both capable of lyricism about bicycles. Moran, it would seem, is like an earlier stage of Molloy, telling the tale of how he began a good bourgeois, parish priest and all, and became a bum. Molloy's tale is of how a bum became a casualty, and it has even been suggested that Molloy is Moran, a later stage of Moran, and that the two parts of the novel have been transposed from their chronological order, the whole tracing one man's descent from garden and wicker chair to utter alienation. This suggestion contains a truth, that Moran at the end of his episode is as disoriented as Molloy at the beginning of his, but it is nevertheless surely false since it reduces Beckett's most powerful effect to the level of a trick. For the eerie power of the book arises surely from the mysterious hold of Molloy, whom he has never seen, on Moran's imagination, and the mysterious psychic disintegration that is perhaps a consequence of this hold, or perhaps its accidental concomitant. It is as though preoccupation with Molloy has power to make the familiar liaisons with familiar reality dissolve; as though Molloy is rather a myth than a character, with a myth's hold on its believers.

As, during his surveillance of A and C, we might have mistaken Molloy for a detective, so at the beginning of Moran's narrative we are entitled on much better evidence to think of him as an operative of some kind. A certain Gaber comes and gives him instructions, reads them to him in fact, but does not suffer him to retain them in written form. This is routine. We do not hear these instructions, but it is evident that the Organization, small or large Moran does not know, has enjoined him to find Molloy. Molloy is surely not worth anyone's trouble, but this is not gone into. (In Occupied France many persons were being sought who were not on the face of it worth anyone's trouble.)

Gaber is 'a messenger'. The Greek for 'messenger' is *angelos*, and the name of a well-known angel is Gabriel. We shall do well to make little of this. Like the hints of detective-story format, it is one of Beckett's devices for imparting to the narrative a sense of near-familiarity, near-intelligibility. To hint at numerous patterns that do not really fit, that will certainly not fit the way the *Odyssey* can be fitted to *Ulysses*, is a device among many for installing us in a world that dissolves. It resembles the inconsequence into which paragraphs lapse, with no loss of grip on the rigorous local clarity of terms and sentences, or the arbitrariness that characterizes Moran's actions just when we are beginning to suppose that we understand them and him.

No sooner has 'the Molloy affair' begun than Moran's self-control is faltering. Within a few pages he is making plans out of their proper order ('I was losing my head already'); two more pages and he is receiving communion without having properly fasted, compromising as he does so his disagreeable piety (he is a loveless man) in a manner expressive of how much he is by now contriving to shut out of his mind. The dialogue with the priest is wonderfully perfunctory:

It's this, I said, Sunday for me without the Body and Blood is like—. He raised his hand. Above all no profane comparisons, he said. Perhaps he was thinking of the kiss without a moustache or beef without mustard. I dislike being interrupted. I sulked. Say no more, he said, a wink is as good as a nod, you want communion. I bowed my head. It's a little unusual, he said. I wondered if he had fed. I knew he was given to prolonged fasts, by way of mortification certainly, and then because his doctor advised it. Thus he killed two birds with one stone. Not a word to a soul, he said, let it remain between us and—. He broke off, raising a finger, and his eyes, to the ceiling. Heavens, he said, what is that stain? I looked in turn at the ceiling. Damp, I said. Tut tut, he said, how annoying. The words tut tut seemed to me the maddest I had heard. There are times, he said, when one feels like weeping. . . .

And communion is given and received in the following spirit:

He came back with a kind of portable pyx, opened it and despatched me without an instant's hesitation. I rose and thanked him warmly. Pah! he said, it's nothing. Now we can talk.

Such is Moran, or such at any rate is Moran within an hour of having heard of Molloy. He abuses his son—this appears to be routine, he does it so often to so little protest. They set out; his instructions begin to fade in his mind, not long after he has told us with the confidence of habit that he will be able to recover their minutest details at will; he undergoes leg pains; loses son, bicycle and money; is reduced to lying on the ground, and crawling; is summoned home, to find his bees and hens dead, his house deserted; and as we take our leave of him he is preparing to set out into the world on crutches ('Perhaps I shall meet Molloy'). His health is now approximately Molloy's health when Molloy began his own quest; the end of the novel thus nearly joins the beginning.

There are other oddities. He meets a man with a heavy coat and a striking hat and a stick, who corresponds, as far as these details go, with the man Molloy sighted so long ago and denominated C, the man who set out 'alone, by unknown ways, in the gathering night, with a stick'. Is it C? We cannot say. If it is C, then C has surely disintegrated too, for the man Moran meets has 'a huge shock of dirty snow-white hair', and begs for bread. On the other hand, we have no assurance that C, when Molloy saw him, would not have displayed such hair had he taken off his hat; we have only, from Molloy, the impression of C's well-groomed self-possession. For that matter, the man Moran meets somewhat resembles his anticipation of Molloy, 'hirsute, craggy and grimacing'. It is Molloy? But we have no reason to suppose that Moran's anticipation of Molloy is accurate, nor have we any record of Molloy's encountering anyone who resembles Moran.

Not long afterward Moran meets a man who resembles himself, enquiring after an old man with a stick. Is it the same old man? And is this another operative like Moran himself, not yet disintegrated? Is this perhaps even A? He kills this man. It is the most perfunctory killing in literature, occurring as it does in the interval between two sentences. 'He thrust his hand at me. . . . I do not know what happened then. But a little later, perhaps a long time later, I found him stretched on the ground, his head in a pulp. I am sorry I cannot indicate more clearly how this result was obtained, it would have been something worth reading.'

This is a valuable emblem of the book. There is never an obscure sentence. Absolute precision, absolute, almost finicky certainty attends the grip of these sentences upon meaning. And yet the uncertainties occur, and pervade, as a house might be in a state of dilapidation without one beam sagging nor one post crumpled. And if we inspect the opening and the closing sentences of Moran's report, the dilapidation of the intervening structure appears nearly absolute. His narrative begins, 'It is midnight. The rain is beating on the windows. I am calm. All is sleeping. Nevertheless I get up and go to my desk.' The narrative ends, 'Then I went back into the house and wrote, It is midnight. The rain is beating on the windows. It was not midnight. It was not raining.'

MALONE DIES

'Malone', writes Malone, 'is what I am called now.' Some pages later he indicates that 'the Murphys, Merciers, Molloys, Morans, Malones' were all beings of his devising. He created, he killed. 'How many have I killed, hitting them on the head or setting fire to them?' He manages to think of five, who would include Murphy and the retired butler in *Murphy*; the *agent* in *Mercier et Camier*; the enquirer killed by Moran, and the charcoal-burner assaulted by Molloy, both in *Molloy* (assuming, that is, that the charcoal-burner died, for we have no testimony to this). Malone is now dying himself, and whiling away the time as before with stories. He calls himself an octogenarian, and speaks of having lived thirty thousand odd days, which would make him at least eighty-two. His plan for the narrative he is starting to write, sitting in bed in an obscure place with an exercise-book and a pencil, is to describe his present state, to tell himself four—on reconsideration, three—stories, to inventory his possessions, to die. His death and the end of his narrative will necessarily synchronize. The fact that he will not be able to describe his death becomes, however, a paradigmatic fact, for he is unable to carry out any other element of the plan. The account of his present state is intermittent, elusive

and contradictory, the stories telescope into one, or possibly
two, and the inventory of his possessions, a luxury he promises
himself, occurs prematurely ('Quick quick my possessions')
and seems not to be completed, the expected pleasure of nume-
rate certainty dwindling into distracted quibbles. The book
ends as he is slaughtering the characters in his story. Is he
himself dead? Is some remoter author slaughtering him?
Has he merely lost strength, or interest, not life? But he has
no life, never had; he is simply the person we intuit when a
hundred or more pages of highly idiosyncratic words claim
that a person is behind them. For words always make such a
claim. Where else would they come from, if not from a person?

It is clear that *Molloy* and *Malone Dies* were conceived as
companion books. '*Cette fois-ci, puis encore une je pense, puis
c'en sera fini je pense*,' runs the opening of Molloy's narrative in
the French edition published in 1951, and *Malone Meurt* was
published in the same year. 'This time, then once more I think,
then I think it'll be over.' It was two years later that *L'Innommable* appeared, to make the trilogy, and when the English
Molloy was published in 1955 Beckett revised this sentence to
entail not two but three tellings. This appears to mean that
though *L'Innommable* existed in manuscript in 1951, Beckett
had either not decided whether he would publish it, or at any
rate not decided whether the three books made a trilogy, though
he had long known that the first two made a duet.

It is helpful, at any rate, for the reader of *Malone Dies* to
bear *Molloy* in mind, since the analogy between the two will
keep his attention focussed on dualities of structure, and both
books work by dividings into two. As *Molloy* is divided between
Molloy's and Moran's consciousness and between their con-
secutive narratives, so different to start with yet so oddly con-
vergent, *Malone Dies* alternates between Malone's 'present
state' (always shifting, because days pass) and the story he is
amusing himself with; and the two, though they start quite
differently, also converge, so that the hero of the story is eventually as old as Malone and confined to a similar room. The
story, moreover, is itself twofold, the hero having apparently

changed names part way, from Sapo (*homo sapiens*) to Macmann (son of man), as it were by analogy with Molloy and
Malone.

Sapo, properly Saposcat (Gk. *skatos*, of or concerning dung)
is a frigid brat, boring to his creator ('What tedium', subjoins
Malone after only two paragraphs). 'He was the eldest child
of poor and sickly parents,' and we are treated to a long paragraph on their poor and sickly aspirations. Saposcat *père*
might get more money working longer hours, but lacks the
strength. They might obviate the need for thoughts about
more money by growing vegetables, but need manure, which
costs money they do not have. 'Nothing remained but to
envisage a smaller house. But we are cramped as it is, said
Mrs Saposcat. And it was an understood thing that they would
be more and more so with every passing year until the day
came when, the departure of the first-born compensating the
arrival of the new-born, a kind of equilibrium would be attained. Then little by little the house would empty. And at
last they would be all alone, with their memories. It would
be time enough then to move. He would be pensioned off,
she at her last gasp. They would take a cottage in the country
where, having no further need of manure, they could afford
to buy it in cartloads. And their children, grateful for the
sacrifices made on their behalf, would come to their assistance.
It was in this atmosphere of unbridled dream that these con-
ferences usually ended. It was as though the Saposcats drew
the strength to live from the prospect of their impotence.'

As for little Sapo, 'At least his health is good, said Mr Saposcat. Not all that, said his wife. But no definite disease, said
Mr Saposcat. A nice thing that would be, at his age, said his
wife.' 'What tedium', indeed. Yet Sapo, though a simpleton
who cannot tell one bird or one tree from another, soon shows
signs of acquiring a life of his own. When he commits a fault
that would merit expulsion from school, and yet is not expelled,
Malone breaks off to remark that he has not been able to find
out why Sapo was not expelled, quite as if Sapo had resources
that are hidden from the man who seems to be making him

up. That is no doubt why Malone continues to recount the
fortunes of Sapo; Sapo, who started out by being a puppet,
now possesses the fascinations of autonomy. If you are amusing
yourself with a fictional character you do not advance the
excitement by making him remain motionless, often standing,
for hours on end; but if you *encounter* a boy who behaves like
that, even if you encounter him in your thoughts, then he is
not without a certain allure. 'People wondered what he could
brood on thus, hour by hour,' and Malone seems to be won-
dering too.

His father supposed him a prey to the first flutterings of sex. At sixteen I was the same, he would say. At sixteen you were earning your
living, said his wife. So I was, said Mr Saposcat. But in the view of
his teachers the signs were rather those of besottedness pure and
simple. Sapo dropped his jaw and breathed through his mouth. It
is not easy to see in virtue of what this expression is incompatible
with erotic thoughts. But indeed his dream was less of girls than of
himself, his own life, his life to be. That is more than enough to stop
up the nose of a lucid and sensitive boy, and cause his jaw temporarily
to sag.

'We are getting on,' comments Malone. 'Nothing is less like
me than this patient, reasonable child, struggling all alone for
years to shed a little light upon himself, avid of the last gleam,
a stranger to the joys of darkness. Here truly is the air I needed,
a lively tenuous air, far from the nourishing murk that is killing me.' He introduces more characters, the Lamberts, equally
devoid of charm. Big Lambert is a pig-sticker by vocation,
and his evening conversation ('to his near and dear ones, while
the lamp burned low') is solely of the last pig he has slaughtered.
The only reported utterances of his overworked wife are 'angry
unanswerable questions, such as, What's the use?' Sapo lingers
among them, silent, unnoticed, staring, as though turning into
an illiterate Murphy. He watches their incompetent burial of
a mule. ('Together they dragged the mule by the legs to the
edge of the hole and heaved it in, on its back. The forelegs,
pointing towards heaven, projected above the level of the
ground. Old Lambert banged them down with his spade.')

There is little incident, little interest, and yet a thread of tenuous interest holds Malone: the thought of Sapo, who could not glide away 'because his movements were rather those of one floundering in a quag', the thought of Sapo, awkward and bizarre, pausing to stare down at the earth, 'blind to its beauty, and to its utility, and to the little wild many-coloured flowers happy among the crops and weeds'. This thought draws Malone back to his own boyhood, and to an evocation of remembered sounds:

Then in my bed, in the dark, on stormy nights, I could tell one from another, in the outcry without, the leaves, the boughs, the groaning trunks, even the grasses and the house that sheltered me. Each tree has its own cry, just as no two whispered alike, when the air was still. .... The sound I liked best had nothing noble about it. It was the barking of the dogs, at night, in the clusters of hovels up in the hills, where the stone-cutters lived, like generations of stone-cutters before them. It came down to me where I lay, in the house in the plain, wild and soft, at the limit of earshot, soon weary. The dogs of the valley replied with their gross bay all fangs and jaws and foam. . . .

This is, as distinct from the paragraphs that synthesize Sapo, a flow of genuine sap, tapped deep down where his most real feelings are buried. Feeling is buried very deep in Malone, and it is fascinating to watch its sudden eloquence, stirred as if by accident. The self on top now is the self of a loveless old man, but he has not quite killed deeper selves. That is perhaps one meaning of the title: his life has been a long dying, not yet terminated, of a boy once fully alive there.

There is sometimes an incident, as when he loses his pencil. There is sometimes another, as when he loses his stick. ('That is the outstanding event of the day.' What days!) Even this loss yields more than we'd think. He lost it trying to wield it like a punt-pole, to propel his bed on its castors (if it has any) through the door 'and even down the stairs, if there is a stairs that goes down'. That is like a boy's fantasy. The man's part is to meditate on the stick, like Swift meditating on a broomstick. 'It is thus that man distinguishes himself from the ape and rises, from discovery to discovery, ever higher, towards the light': there is no mistaking the sardonic bitterness of this estimate of the man's mature estate. Another incident: a man comes in, hits him on the head to waken him, then stands by his bed unspeaking for seven hours, with a break for lunch. This is human fellowship, so far as we are shown it. Malone draws up a list of twenty-one written questions in case the man returns, but he does not.

The lights fade and shift, the room seems to alter, certainly his body alters.

All strains towards the nearest deeps, and notably my feet, which even in the ordinary way are so much further from me than all the rest, from my head I mean, for that is where I am fled, my feet are leagues away. And to call them in, to be cleaned for example, would I think take me over a month, exclusive of the time required to locate them. Strange, I don't feel my feet any more, my feet feel nothing any more, and a mercy it is. And yet I feel they are beyond the range of the most powerful telescope. Is that what is known as having a foot in the grave?

But more important than any of these 'present state' happenings, the story gathers momentum. Sapo wanders off and is found by his creator ('I have taken a long time to find him again, but I have found him. How did I know it was he, I don't know.') A good question, since even his name has changed; he is now Macmann, son of Man, an aged wanderer, even as Molloy. He is telling himself a story, 'the kind of story he has been telling himself all his life, saying, This cannot possibly last much longer.' So his growing resemblance to Malone is unmistakable. Then he passes out of sight rolling, like Molloy crawling; comes to in 'a kind of asylum' (is that the kind of place Malone is now?); then—O wonder!—he undergoes a love story, for his place of repose is peopled, as Malone's seems not to be.

The lady is Moll, another inmate, 'immoderately ill-favoured of both face and body'. There springs up gradually between her and Macmann, we are told, a kind of intimacy, of which they attempt a physical translation. But, 'given their age and scant experience of carnal love, it was natural that they should not succeed, at first shot, in giving each other the impression that they were made for each other.' Nevertheless, 'far from losing heart, they warmed to their work. And though both were completely impotent they finally succeeded, summoning to their aid all the resources of the skin, the mucus and the imagination, in striking from their dry and feeble clips a kind of sombre gratification. So that Moll exclaimed, being (at that stage) the more expansive of the two, Oh would we had but met sixty years ago! But on the long road to this what flutterings, alarms and bashful fumblings, of which only this, that they gave Macmann some insight into the meaning of the expression, Two is company.'

This is one more of the resonant passages. From beneath the wilful grotesquerie of his fiction, the buried Malone, the Malone of feeling, is nearly breaking forth. 'In striking from their dry and feeble clips a kind of sombre gratification': Beckett has nowhere any finer sentence, though many as fine. It is no sombre gratification that such language yields; its clips, far from dry and feeble, touch on noble resources of eloquence, Vergilian in their amber evocation of the sorrowful, the futile, the ever-hopeful. And that is the peculiarity of this book, in contrast with *Molloy*, that it rises to such extraordinary heights. At best the feeling in *Molloy* is mellow, elegiac. Malone is capable of starker rages, more conscious wit, and more impressive peaks. 'Two is company', a seeming tautology, is human wisdom, the meaning of which each man must discover, if at all, for himself. Sardonic though the pedantry with which he quotes it, Malone is heartbreakingly close, at such times, to the liberty that comports with such understanding.

Malone, though, has he ever gained insight into the meaning of this expression? We cannot say. More to the point, we cannot tell that he has not. His company, here, now, is perforce mental: Macmann, Moll, sundry lunatics, a Lady Pedal who enjoins the lunatics in the story to 'Sing! Make the most of this glorious day!' and a Lemuel who goes about at the end dispatching them with a hatchet, for no reason except that

Malone seems tired of them. Malone's possessions included a photograph concerning which he worked up some delicacies of feeling.

It is not a photograph of me, but I am perhaps at hand. It is an ass, taken from in front and close up, at the edge of the ocean, it is not the ocean, but for me it is the ocean. They naturally tried to make it raise its head, so that its beautiful eyes might be impressed on the celluloid, but it holds it lowered. You can tell by its ears that it is not pleased. They put a boater on its head. The thin hard parallel legs, the little hooves light and dainty on the sand. The outline is blurred, that's the operator's giggle shaking the camera.

These are cautious affections that Malone is indulging. Turning his attention to his story, he reflects, 'Moll, I'm going to kill her.' He does. In the story she dies, not without undergoing a loss of hair such that 'she confessed to Macmann that she did not dare comb it any more, for fear of making it fall out even faster. He said to himself with satisfaction, She tells me everything.' And a photograph survives her. Are we to connect this photograph, Malone's fantasy, with the photograph of the ass, which he really possessed, and with his evident affection for 'the little hooves light and dainty on the sand'?

Macmann carried with him and contemplated from time to time the photograph that Moll had given him. . . . She was standing beside a chair and squeezing in her hands her long plaits. Traces were visible, behind her, of a kind of trellis with clambering flowers. . . . When giving this keep-sake to Macmann she had said, I was fourteen, I well remember the day, a summer day, it was my birthday, afterwards they took me to see Punch and Judy. . . . Diligently Moll pressed her lips together, in order to hide her great buck-teeth. The roses must have been pretty, they must have scented the air. In the end Macmann tore up this photograph and threw the bits in the air, one windy day. Then they scattered, though all subjected to the same conditions, as though with alacrity.

Why does Macmann tear up the photograph? We may perhaps reflect that he never knew *that* Moll. We may also reflect that he is a projection of his author, Malone, he of 'I'm going to kill her'. And kill everyone else he does, so far as he can, within ten more pages; and the last words are,

never anything

there

any more

How loveless is Malone, how dryly jaunty, how miserable, how funny. The man who conceived the notion of poling his bed down the stairs has a claim on our sympathies, as con-geners of Columbus and Galileo, that one would never predict from his misanthropies alone. He is one of the most engaging of the Beckett twilight men. The book has not a dull page, not even when its subject is dullness, and we nearly do not notice how the lethal rages that shake the man before us bespeak a quiescent monster who was long ago otherwise.

THE UNNAMABLE

The Unnamable—so named because, at the simplest level of meaning, he does not know who he may be and hopes to find out—sits nowhere, nowhen, 'like a great horned owl in an aviary', grinding his 'wordy-gurdy'. 'I am in my mother's room', began Molloy. 'Where now?' begins the newest voice.

Can it be . . . that one day I simply stayed in, in where, instead of go-ing out, in the old way, out to spend day and night as far away as pos-sible, it wasn't far. Perhaps that is how it began. You think you are simply resting the better to act when the time comes, and you soon find yourself powerless ever to do anything again. No matter how it happened. I say it, not knowing what. . . .

That is as much of an explanation as we are going to get. One can imagine Murphy, one day, simply staying in. But the pure bliss of Murphy was banished from Beckett's cosmos long ago, as was the reader's pure bliss which entails knowing exactly what is happening and just who did what to whom. For the explanation that has been provisionally offered, that we are hearing from a man who formerly went out but one one day simply decided to stay in, will fade very quickly as many multiplied words make his situation more and more mysterious and distressing. Thus shortly he is talking of the compulsion to string out words, likening it to a pensum, an imposition of lines to be written out as a punishment for in-accurately repeating a lesson. Yet he does not know what lines he is to write out, and can only hope to hit on the right ones by chance. And when he has completed the pensum he will still have the lesson to repeat, and will have to rely on chance to get that right also. 'Strange notion in any case, and eminently open to suspicion, that of a task to be performed, before one can be at rest. Strange task, which consists in speak-ing of oneself. Strange hope, turned towards silence and peace.'

All this is provisional, hypothetical; yet, he says, 'Let us suppose . . . that it is in fact required of me that I say some-thing, something that is not to be found in all I have said up to now.' 'All I have said up to now' includes the previous fictions of Samuel Beckett. 'All these Murphys, Molloys and Malones do not fool me. They have made me waste my time, suffer for nothing, speak of them when, in order to stop speak-ing, I should have spoken of me and me alone.' For the goal is to stop speaking. We are veering close to the Gestapo theme: the theme of the man who is required to talk, and in fact does not possess the information his tormentors must be made to think they have extracted. They will leave him alone, he may conjecture, if he has the aplomb for conjecture, when by accident he hits on something plausible.

When all goes silent, and comes to an end, it will be because the words have been said, those it behoved me to say, no need to know which, no means of knowing which, they'll be there somewhere, in the heap, in the torrent, not necessarily the last, they have to be ratified by the proper authority, that takes time, he's far from here, they bring him the verbatim report of the proceedings, once in a way, he knows the words that count. . . .

And while word goes back and forth to the proper authority, the monologue must necessarily go on. Perhaps the requisite words have already been spoken? If so, how long will it be before the speaker knows?

Still less than *Godot*, though, is this an 'Occupation' book, for the writer's impulse to write is another of its themes, a mysterious theme, and everyone's impulse to talk, and the need of the mind to remain in action whether it has anything to engage it or not. We have thoughts *of* something; we also have thoughts that find something to be about, many things successively to be about, as in the 'stream of consciousness'. And again, there is thought that barely ticks over, like an idling motor, propelling nothing, barely consuming fuel, but constituting the life of the thinking faculty. *The Unnamable* is its trace, sour at being disturbed and being compelled to find something to be *of*, turner over of word after barely differentiated word, anxious only to be left in peace, unscrutinized. When you think to ask what you are thinking of, then, perhaps, you turn the harrowing spotlight on to The Unnamable.

He faces back to a past spent inventing the previous characters—'a ponderous chronicle of moribunds in their courses, moving, clashing, writhing or fallen in shortlived swoons'—and forward to a future in which 'perhaps I shall be obliged, in order not to peter out, to invent another fairytale, yet another, with heads, trunks, arms, legs and all that follows, let loose in the changeless round of imperfect shadow and dubious light.' He is represented, fraudulently, 'up there in the world', by someone he first calls Basil, then decides to call Mahood. He has a future state, still more reduced, if he can succeed in getting it born, and this he calls Worm: 'Worm the inexpugnable', the Undying Worm.

He starts to tell a story about Mahood, the one-legged man,

which quickly, imperceptibly, turns into a story about himself, drawing on Mahood's testimony. He is moving, on his crutches, in an excruciating slow converging spiral with his numerous next-of-kin at its core, circling back from a worldwide sweep. They chatter, they comment, they restrain one another from distracting him with shouts of encouragement. 'Often the cry went up, He's down! But in reality I had sunk to the ground of my own free will, in order to be rid of my crutches and have both hands available to minister to myself in peace and comfort. Admittedly it is difficult, for a man with but one leg, to sink to earth in the full force of the expression, particularly when he is weak in the head and the sole surviving leg flaccid for want of exercise, or from excess of it. The simplest thing then is to fling away the crutches and collapse. That is what I did.' The old folk all die of ptomaine, while he tramples them without rancour. Is he there now, at that decaying centre? Is that where 'here' is?

In the next Mahood story, Mahood is the man in the jar, armless and legless, across from a restaurant. The situation is elaborated in fantastic detail; the menu is affixed to the jar for passers-by to read, and the proprietress regards Mahood as 'an undeniable asset'. She has festooned his jar with Chinese lanterns to enhance its advertisement value. 'Yes, I represent for her a tidy little capital and, if I should ever happen to die, I am convinced she would be genuinely annoyed. This should help me to live.'

In fact Mahood (and again 'I' and Mahood seem inextricable) is growing less embodied, rounder, more Platonic, rather like The Unnamable in whatever may be his present state. The narrative, if that is what it is, begins to teeter about the fulcrum of the Cartesian 'ergo'. I think, that is (alas) plain. Descartes went on smartly, 'therefore I am'. But am I, can I even come into existence? For ten pages we follow the effort of Worm to get born, an imperfectly satisfactory event. After a descant on being made of words (anyone in a book is made of words), a new surrogate emerges, simply 'I', acquiring as it struggles into being the requisite accessories:

There I am in any case equipped with eyes, which I open and shut, two, perhaps blue, knowing it avails nothing, for I have a head now too, where all manner of things are known, can it be of me I'm speaking, is it possible, of course not, that's another thing I know, I'll speak of me when I speak no more.

This 'I' requires a name but does not receive one; panic is mounting; sentences grow longer and longer; the need is to be formed and defined and named, the anticipation is always of rebirth, the horror is when the birth occurs. Now Mahood is well in the past, as is apparently Worm; now the compulsion itself to narrate, narrate grows clearer, more insistent. 'Yes, in my life, since we must call it so, there were three things, the inability to speak, the inability to be silent, and solitude, that's what I've had to make the best of.' He proposes some words on the silence. And a terminal five-page sentence ends with the possibility that the end is yet one more beginning:

... perhaps they [the words] have carried me to the threshold of my story, before the door that opens on my story, that would surprise me, if it opens, it will be I, it will be the silence, where I am, I don't know, I'll never know, in the silence you don't know, you must go on, I can't go on, I'll go on.

A difficult book, a Zero book? Certainly the book that, of all the fictions we have in the world, most cruelly reduces the scope of incident, the wealth of character. The utmost austerity has never dreamed of going so far. 'I have lost my stick', wrote the dying Malone, 'That is the outstanding event of the day', aware, Malone, that he is committing to paper a humour of disproportion; aware that in properly conducted works of fiction, such as he is not essaying, outstanding events are of ampler magnitude. He is having his little joke. But, 'Air, the air', writes The Unnamble, 'is there anything to be squeezed from that old chestnut?' and we have what very nearly qualifies, in this book, as an event, the wit that transforms 'old chestnut' from a figure of speech into something squeezable (but spiky), performing a scrutable *deed*, but without humour, without pleasure. He is squeezing old chestnuts, worrying old dead themes, with heroic pertinacity, and with no such wink as Malone's, no pleasure such as Malone's in contemplating the Homeric splendours to which his incidents do not measure up. No, weary persistence, like the low vitality of the heart that beats during surgery, is setting sentence after sentence with unwavering punctilio, and it is with a bitter rictus that he contemplates the possibility of things getting livelier ('one never knows, does one, no'). 'Perhaps Mahood will emerge from his urn and make his way towards Montmartre, on his belly, singing, I come, I come, my heart's delight.' Small likelihood! And what a bitter effort it took to imagine even so much, even for a sentence's span.

For the theme of the book is heroism without drama: the heroism of the man undergoing torture, by nothing as dramatic as a Gestapo but by *accidie*, and having no recourse to Seconal or lewd imaginings. Flaubert envisioned a book which should be about Nothing, a book with no content, held together by the sheer style; but Nothing came rather easily to Flaubert, and as for style, he knew how to work for it. It would even have been, such a book, a self-indulgence. *The Unnamable* is far from self-indulgent, if only because the calm excellence of the writing shows no trace of narcissism; he accords himself no such pleasure.

'The sun shone, having no alternative, upon the nothing new.' That is the first sentence of *Murphy*, and it invokes Nothing, and it is rather well pleased with itself. But the marvellous precisions of *The Unnamable* own no such taint. 'I, of whom I know nothing, I know my eyes are open, because of the tears that pour from them unceasingly.' No self-appreciation enhaloes the three I's, not even though the second is discriminated from the first and third in a manner to afford a philosopher *frisson*. 'I know I am seated, my hands on my knees, because of the pressure against my rump, against the soles of my feet, against the palms of my hands, against my knees.' This exhausts the list of pressures, and does so with finesse, but the finesse neither baits the reader as do the lists in *Watt*, nor expresses its own difficulty as do some of the enumerations in *Molloy*. 'Against my palms the pressure is of my knees, against my knees of my palms, but what is it that presses against my rump, against the soles of my feet? I don't know. My spine is not supported.' This exhausts the analysis of pressures. 'I mention these details to make sure I am not lying on my back, my legs raised and bent, my eyes closed. It is well to establish the position of the body at the outset, before passing on to more important matters.' This is grimly humorous, positing a maxim for which it is difficult to think of another application. Can this be said to be a maxim, if it has not some breadth of applicability? Yet it has the air of a maxim. Such penumbrae of logic, not dwelt on, are The Unnamable's little pleasures. But he never wavers in formulating, one by one, those beautifully shaped and balanced sentences, of perfect local clearness. Nor does he panic when uncertainty, or consternation, prolongs the sentences, accumulating phrases set off by commas.

Is the declarative sentence perhaps man's highest achievement? It may well be. No brute frames one. The uncivilized do no more than merely *name*, remaining at the mercy of the namable, or express by grunts and roars their pleasures and pains. The declarative sentence, then, which detaches from the big blooming buzzing confusion this thing, this subject, *this*, suavely validated by centuries of agreement and by dictionaries, and predicates with the aid of that mysterious agent the verb, to answer human desire, human satisfaction, creating a molecule of thought, a microcosm: in an absence of blooming and buzzing it can remain man's stay, excerpting, predicating. And always quoting; for all the words are old words, and all the phrases; it is something, if you are as horribly alone as The Unnamable, to know that comfort. 'Ah yes', he says, 'I am truly bathed in tears', recognizing like an old friend a familiar expression, never till now of literal applicability. ('For I feel my tears coursing over my chest, my sides, and all down my back.') That is truly what it is to be bathed in tears; it is like Macmann gaining some insight into the expression, two is company. Language is this man's bitter company, grinding at his wordy-gurdy, in a book about

Nothing that does not lose its power to fascinate, because the Nothing is being combatted by a moral quality: by the minimal courage that utters, utters, utters, without moan, without solecism.

8 Stories and Texts for Nothing

The uncertainties of *Watt* are uncertainties of evidence. In all Beckett's subsequent non-dramatic work, the reader is made to share uncertainties of a different order, the uncertainties of the first person; these include those of memory, and those of authorship. As being his first venture in the mode he was to exploit so richly, the three *Stories* repay close attention.[10] They date from 1945, though their French publication came just after the trilogy of novels and their English versions more than a decade later still. In all three a narrator, always on the move, is struggling with the superficies of mundane existence, shelter, food, diversion; not striving to execute any specific purpose, but staying alive because he is alive.

In addition to the first person and its vagaries—the inability to remember facts, the uncertainty as to why he is narrating at all, the loss of heart when set-pieces seem called for ('Only the ground-floor windows—no, I can't')—two other Beckett conventions at least are introduced: the narrator's gradual reduction to vagrancy, and the resemblance of his world to that of silent films.

Thus *The Expelled* opens with the hero flying through the air, having been ejected through a front door from which steps descend. During his trajectory he has the wit to execute a piece of reasoning which he concludes 'before coming to rest in the gutter', where a bang arouses him, 'my hands flat on the sidewalk and my legs braced for flight'. How many of the great cinematic mimes have been photographed in just that position! It was a speciality of Buster Keaton's. But the bang

is the door slamming after a second ejection, that of his hat,
which sails towards him through the air, rotating. He catches
it and puts it on; it appears to be his hallmark. (Keaton, Chaplin,
Lloyd, all were hallmarked by hats; later everyone in *Godot*
will wear a bowler.) His walk too hallmarks him:

I set off. What a gait. Stiffness of the lower limbs, as if nature had
denied me knees, extraordinary splaying of the feet to right and left
of the line of march. The trunk, on the contrary, as if by the effect
of a compensatory mechanism, was as flabby as an old ragbag, tossing
wildly to the unpredictable jolts of the pelvis. I have often tried to
correct these defects, to stiffen my bust, flex my knees, and walk with
my feet in front of one another, for I had at least five or six, but it always
ended in the same way, I mean by a loss of equilibrium, followed by
a fall.

From this highly specifiable identity he descends gradually—
assuming that all three stories, *The Expelled, The Calmative*,
and *The End* treat of the same man—until at the end of *The
End*, in another Keatonian detail, he is foundering at sea, in
a leaky boat, chained for some reason by his waist to its bow,
though unlike the great mimes, all of whose reflexes ministered
to survival as their intellects assuredly did not, he seems to
have made the hole in the boat himself, and is putting up no
struggle. Shortly before this we find him attempting to milk
a cow into his hat. 'Clutching the dug with one hand I kept
my hat under it with the other. But in the end she prevailed.
For she dragged me across the threshold and out into the giant
streaming ferns, where I was forced to let go.' He reflects that
he had not thought 'our cows too could be so inhuman'.

Most of the incidents are less exceptional. Beckett's care has
been to make the most ordinary encounters seem as bizarre as
these, partly by stressing the naiveté of a protagonist to whom
trivia are perpetual astonishments, partly by a crispness of
denotation that makes every detail start forth as though edge-
lighted.

My bench was still there. It was shaped to fit the curves of the seated
body. It stood beside a watering trough, gift of a Mrs Maxwell to the
city horses, according to the inscription. During the short time I

rested there several horses took advantage of this monument. The iron shoes approached and the jingle of the harness. Then silence. That was the horse looking at me. Then the noise of pebbles and mud that horses make when drinking. Then the silence again. That was the horse looking at me again. Then the pebbles again. Then the silence again. Till the horse had finished drinking or the driver deemed it had drunk its fill. The horses were uneasy. Once, when the noise stopped, I turned and saw the horse looking at me. The driver too was looking at me. Mrs Maxwell would have been pleased if she could have seen her trough rendering such services to the city horses.

Such is the narrative texture that none of the stories depends on a 'plot', or a 'point'. All that happens in the first is a day spent wandering and a night spent in a stable, and led on though we are irresistibly from sentence to sentence, we are not prevented from reflecting that nothing more happens. All that happens in the second, which seems to entail a spell of hospitalization, is a bedridden man's story of encounters that seem hallucinatory and close amid a swoon with the lucidity of hallucination. All that happens in the third is an indigent's progress toward that leaking boat. The three span a descent from middle-class somnambulistic orthodoxy to the fluid expedients of beggardom, traversed with neither surprise nor rancour, and with never a backward glance.

   Out of these stories, out of their procedures, grew *Molloy* and *Malone Dies*. Out of *The Unnamable* came the *Texts for Nothing*, thirteen of them, which Beckett published in French and English in the same volumes with the *Stories*. They may be characterized as the efforts of an 'I' who has the ambiguous existence of a tired author's figment to ascertain who he is and what he is meant to be doing, not that he has the strength to be doing anything, nor the coherence to sustain an identity. 'Where would I go, if I could go, who would I be, if I could be, what would I say, if I had a voice, who says this, saying it's me?' This is from Text IV, where the character's dissatisfaction with his author is uppermost.

. . . he would like it to be my fault that words fail him, of course words fail him. He tells his story every five minutes, saying it is not his, there's cleverness for you. He would like it to be my fault that he has no story, of course he has no story, that's no reason for trying to foist one on me . . . . If at least he would dignify me with the third person, like his other figments, not he, he'll be satisfied with nothing less than me, for his me. . . . That's how he speaks, this evening, how he has me speak, how he speaks to himself, how I speak, there is only me. . . .

This quotation suggests as helpful a way to think of the sequence as any, though it hasn't by any means explicit applicability to all of the thirteen Texts. They may equally well be read, most of them, as fantasies of non-being. In an especially bizarre one he beholds an empty costume moving: first a white stick and an ear-trumpet, then 'a bowler. hat which seems to my sorrow a sardonic synthesis of all those that never fitted me and, at the other extremity, a complete pair of brown boots, lacerated and gaping. These insignia, if I may so describe them, advance in concert, as though connected by the traditional human excipient, halt, move on again, confirmed by the vast show-windows.' In another we have a vision of permanent arrest, ticket in hand, in the third-class waiting room of the South-Eastern Railway Terminus, erect and rigid forever while the station lies in ruins. All thirteen are stylistic triumphs; so tart is the phrasing, so calculated are the surprises of diction, that empty though the sentence we are reading may seem it is difficult to refrain from reading the one after it.

The plight of a character waiting on the whims of his author entered nearly a decade later into the composition of that starkest and strangest of all Samuel Beckett's fictions, the Inferno called *How It Is*. Between the *Texts* and *How It Is* came plays, and notably his strangest and starkest play, *Endgame*. So the *Texts* are like *un recul pour mieux sauter*. And after *How It Is* and still more short dramatic works have come very brief evocative compositions, as devoid of 'subject-matter' as the *Texts for Nothing* but stranger, more inventive, in technique. The Text, the short work with no real subject but its own queer cohesion, is a recurrent mode for Beckett's imagination to explore.

9 Endgame

So little here, so much here: and very likely Beckett's most self-sufficient, most economical, most fully realized work. It is one more play for a small theatre, most effective when the theatre is no more than half full and we hear ourselves emit the laughter into which we have been betrayed. And an actor dominates it from beginning to end, an actor granted one of the richest parts in twentieth-century theatre, a part named Hamm, perhaps to remind us of a part named Hamlet, likewise succulent. And an actor is a ham? In colloquial English he is, too often. The play was first written in French, and a French audience would hear no such resonances in 'Hamm', but Beckett has been known to pun across languages before this. 'Bally', for instance, a place-name in *Molloy*, scatological in one dimension, Hibernian in another, is likewise not a penetrable pun for a French reader, yet it is used in the French text.

But—the reader will object—I was arguing on exactly contrary grounds the irrelevance of finding 'God' in 'Godot' because that play too was written in French, and no French word for the deity contains the syllable 'God—'. I was arguing that. But it must be remembered also that the French word 'Godot' does not contain the syllable 'God—'. It contains the syllable 'Go—'. And remember that Hamm and Bally are not French names but alien names; whereas Godot, or Godeau, is a French name. There was a certain Godeau, a bicycle racer, whose career Beckett used to follow in the sporting press; and Paris boasts a Rue Godot de Mauroy; and there is a wonderful story of Samuel Beckett on a flight from Paris to London, being thrown into consternation (remember, here, the Irish regard for omens) by a voice on a cabin loud-speaker from the pilot's compartment, '*Le capitaine Godot vous accorde des bienvenues.*' A plausible French name, then, if not a common one; whereas 'Hamm' would fall on French ears like a dull crepitation, contentless.

Hamm, then, and Clov. Ham and clove? And Nagg and Nell: German *Nagel*, nail, and English nail? Perhaps. And the French for nail is *clou*, in which case 'Hamm' suggests 'hammer'. As so often, we are being teased by hints of system, not to be much pursued. And where is this place? It is here, that is all we can say, here before us, on stage. The set does not *represent*, the set is itself. It has high windows, through which we cannot see, and when Clov mounts his ladder and informs us that there is nothing to be seen, he tells the simple truth, for what can be seen, through stage windows?

But surely (says the reader again) we are to imagine that it is some other place, surrounded by an outdoors, and that when Clov gazes through the windows and sees nothing he is reporting that the outdoors has been consumed by some unimaginable catastrophe? Moreover the text alludes to the room before us as 'the shelter', outside of which is death. Are we not to imagine a fallout shelter, perhaps, and the last hours of the last morsels of human life, after perhaps an H-Bomb explosion? The Bomb was much on the mind of Europe in 1957 when this play was published.

We may imagine such things if we like, because we are given the hints you mention; but we may also imagine that the players are simply *on stage*; thus Hamm speaks of warming up for his last soliloquy, and mentions 'an aside', and Clov says, 'This is what we call making an exit', though he does not make it. Remember, further, that all the world's a stage. Conversely, then, this stage is all the world, including the vanishing world we are taught to imagine when our attention is being averted to catastrophe.

We may collect further hints, further analogies. Hamm is a blind man who tells stories. If we are thinking of Shakespeare,

his blindness is like Lear's. Or he is like Homer, a blind man
who told stories; or like James Joyce, yet another such, and
known to Samuel Beckett, who in conversation dwells on Joyce's
heroism, always in pain, always in tribulation, always doggedly
synthesizing the gaieties of his verbal world. (Though we are
not to find Hamm's fantasies gay.) Or he is like the dying God
of whom we have been hearing ever since Nietzsche: a God
with a demiurge (Clov) who is seeing to the assembly of a dog
and has not completed this work (is God's work ever complete? Ever to be complete?) and a blind God, moreover,
blind and tyrannical, like Fate. Or he is like the mysterious Mr
Knott in *Watt*, who kept servants; a reduced Knott, with a
staff of one, and that one on the point of leaving. Or he is like
Godot.

Godot? What made us think Godot might be beneficent,
benevolent, should he appear? This was perhaps the world
Didi and Gogo sought to enter, and if so then it may be well
that they wait. It is, to return to our starting-point, a stage
world, where the players, as Hamm says, are kept here by 'the
dialogue', and cannot go about their affairs until, every night,
they have recited it, every word, to the end. Theirs is the doom
of perpetual re-enactment, until such time as some faceless
tyrant (the public) shall have lost interest and the run may
close. If this happens soon, the play will be said to have failed
(but the actors will be freed). If it happens late, after many
months perhaps, the play will be deemed a success: the more
successful the longer the players are imprisoned. Hamm, we
are to suppose, is simply kept on stage, in that chair, and his
parents in those trash-cans; and after each night's performance
some hidden power covers them with a sheet until the next night,
to keep off dust. The performance begins, anyhow, with Clov
removing sheets and folding them. First the curtain goes up,
then the sheets are removed, then the cloth uncovers Hamm's
face, then the black glasses come off his eyes: a ritual strip-
tease. And Clov's first words, after the sheets come off but
before the cloth and the glasses, are a longing to be released
from this ritual:

Finished, it's finished, nearly finished, it must be nearly finished.
(*Pause.*)
Grain upon grain, one by one, and one day, suddenly, there's a heap, a little heap, the impossible heap.
(*Pause.*)
I can't be punished any more.

When the grains have become a heap, he will be let off, and when will that be? Sextus Empiricus the Pyrrhonist used just this example to show that the simplest words—words like 'heap'—were in fact empty of meaning. It is like asking when a play may be said to have had a 'run'.

And his time here is a punishment. So was the time of Belacqua, Dante's friend, who was condemned, because of his late repentance, to sit for as many years as he had lived on earth before he might even be admitted to Purgatory. Dante encounters him (*Purg.* IV) lounging in the shade of a rock, 'even as a man settles himself to rest out of laziness', and since he was always slothful it seems a pleasant rest, though he does ask Dante to abridge it with a prayer. This passage caught Beckett's attention early in life. He named the protagonist of his first book, *More Pricks Than Kicks*, Belacqua Shuah. Later he permitted Murphy to contemplate the 'Belacqua bliss', which is the bliss of dreaming again through one's life, at one's ease, without having to *do* again what is dreamed, and Murphy hopes that 'no godly chandler' will shorten his time with a prayer. It is by way of 'the Belacqua bliss' that Murphy ascends to felicity in his rocking-chair. But like so much that is contained in the system of *Murphy*, that pre-war dream is horribly parodied now. Hamm, in his chair, immobile, sightless, is a tormented Murphy, and Clov required to re-enact, re-enact, re-enact, is a tormented Belacqua, and the audience (ourselves) is a collective Jealous God, like the powers that keep The Unnamable wording, until he may hit upon the combination for silence. These themes, still more proper to theatre than to prose, are more explicit in this play than they were in *The Unnamable*, and will be refined yet more in the play called *Play*.

Clov's unmodulated voice is like Lucky's. Hamm, on the
other hand, has the actor's satisfactions, like Pozzo. Pozzo, we
remember, another master with an enslaved servant, performed
in the grand manner, even spraying his throat with a vaporizer
before essaying an especially florid cadenza. Hamm's opening
soliloquy is something for a player to get his teeth into.

Me—
(*he yawns*)
—to play.
(*He holds the handkerchief spread out before him.*)
Old stancher!
[Business with glasses and handkerchief.] (*He clears his throat, and
joins the tips of his fingers.*)
Can there be misery—
(*he yawns*)
—loftier than mine? . . .

'Can there be misery loftier than mine?'—the tragic hero's
self-appreciation. 'And say besides that in Aleppo once . . .'
enjoined Othello, his world down in ruins, engaged, as T. S.
Eliot put it, in 'cheering himself up'. Hamm cheers himself up
with the satisfactions of Style. 'Nicely put, that,' he remarks
of his own remarks; or, 'There's English for you.' It is as if
Othello were to comment on the fine blank verse he is uttering.
(Are his words his own? We are to pretend they are.)

We gather clues to the world's deprivations. There are no
more bicycle-wheels, for instance. There are not even any
bicycles. 'When there were still bicycles', says Clov, 'I wept
to have one. I crawled at your feet. You told me to go to hell.
Now there are none.' For the old man in the trash-can there
is no more pap ('You'll never get any more pap'); and when
Hamm in his lofty misery concludes that Nature has forgotten
us, Clov says, 'There's no more nature.' 'No more nature!
You exaggerate.' 'In the vicinity.'

Even Hamm loses his nerve occasionally.

HAMM: This is not much fun.
           (*Pause.*)
           But that's always the way at the end of the day, isn't it, Clov?

CLOV: Always.
HAMM: It's the end of the day like any other day, isn't it, Clov?
CLOV: Looks like it.
      (*Pause.*)
HAMM: (*anguished*): What's happening, what's happening?
CLOV: Something is taking its course.

Yes, something is taking its course. As sentences go, that is
a sentence. It creates a little order, we may suppose; and later
Clov is to speak of creating a little order, by which he means
clearing everything away. 'I love order. It's my dream. A
world where all would be silent and still and each thing in its
last place, under the last dust.' Order is immobility, or else
absence.

We need not add that theirs is a loveless world. Hamm curses
his father for engendering him, overstepping the limit of Job,
who merely cursed the day of his birth and also the night in
which it was said, There is a man child conceived (though
how anybody was in a position to say that is a thing no scriptural commentator has plausibly explained). Hamm's fantasies
are of posturing while a serf grovels at his feet in an anguish of
concern for a doomed child. ('It was the moment I was waiting
for'—the moment when he can force the father to choose
whether to abandon the child or to share its death.) Hamm's
father curses him; with good reason, considering the life in
which Hamm maintains him. 'I hope the day will come when
you'll really need to have me listen to you, and need to hear
my voice, any voice. (*Pause.*) Yes, I hope I'll live till then,
to hear you calling me like when you were a tiny boy, and were
frightened, in the dark, and I was your only hope.' Yet in those
days, when Hamm was a tiny boy, 'We let you cry. Then we
moved you out of earshot, so that we might sleep in peace.'
It has been a hereditary lovelessness, perhaps, or perhaps we
are to suppose that it is species-specific. (Though 'I had a very
happy childhood,' Beckett once said in response to a question.
Perhaps he is imagining a mutant species.)

Mysteriously, near the end, a child appears outside the windows, or at least Clov says that he does; and just such a child

as figures in Hamm's endless story. 'If he exists,' Hamm says, 'he'll die there or he'll come here. And if he doen't . . . .' And Clov is free to go, and pauses till play's end on the threshold of going, much as Watt was to leave when the new servant arrived. But the child may die out there, or he may not exist. And if he comes in here, he may look forward to the life of a second Clov, to whom, it is conceded, Hamm has been as a father.

At any rate, this Clov gone (or gone so far as Hamm can tell, for Hamm is blind), Hamm utters his last soliloquy, complete with 'a little poetry', the phrasing carefully polished. The final form runs, 'You cried for night; it falls: now cry in darkness', and like God who saw that it was good, he comments, 'Nicely put, that.' Then another haunting cadence: 'Moments for nothing, now as always, time was never and time is over, reckoning closed and story ended.'

And after his final discards, self-deprived of gaff, of dog, of whistle, he concludes grandly with a Stoic resolve to speak no more about it, speak no more. 'Old stancher!'—the handkerchief about to cover his face once more—'You . . . remain.' With his stick and his fantasies he resembles in more than one way the dying Malone, but Malone achieved no curtain-speech.

Endgame, says the title; and Hamm is the King, nearly in check. Is that boy the new servant, or the checking piece? Is Clov, with his odd walk, the Knight, which moves angularly? Are those ashcans rooks? Does all that devastation correspond to pieces removed? No more than the other analogies the text hints at is this analogy, it would seem, meant for rigorous application. Yet to the reader of Beckett's canon it cannot but recall the game Murphy played that night with Mr Endon, before ascending to the chair where he rocked till the 'superfine chaos' of the gas invaded his system. In that game Mr Endon, intent on his symmetrical deployment and retraction of the pieces, ignored opportunity after opportunity to capture a piece of Murphy's, try though Murphy might to entice him with flaunted vulnerability. The game ended with Murphy's pieces (White) in disarray—a 'superfine chaos', in fact—and

Mr Endon's (Black) marched all of them back to a close approximation of the starting array. Murphy's hedonistic rock then ended in gentle annihilation: we are told, in 'peace'.

This game, on the other hand, has been played against no Endon, but against a relentless opponent who has seized each advantage and has stripped the board. That to live is to play a game against a relentless but utterly fair opponent was a metaphor publicized by T. H. Huxley, in the days when nature Red in Tooth and Claw was much on the Victorian mind. Hamm disproves the assertion that there is no more nature by asserting that the work of attrition goes on: 'We breathe, we change! We lose our hair, our teeth! Our bloom! Our ideals!' 'Then she hasn't forgotten us,' is Clov's concession. The desolation in *Endgame*, however, seems more than natural; the sea is abnormally calm, the light grey. And the man in the chair does not rock himself into some Nirvana, for the chair does not rock (it is on castors) and there is no Nirvana. Still, there are dreams ('What dreams! Those forests!') which apparently restore a time when there were forests and when there was what he calls 'love' ('If I could sleep I might make love. I'd go into the woods'). Murphy's dreams at their most satisfactory shut out all the forms of the big world in favour of utter entropic featurelessness. Hamm's big world tends toward entropic featurelessness, and he is glad enough of dreams that restore the old world. The big world, in short, grows like the world Murphy was pleased to imagine, and there is no peace in it, none.

Not that the play depends at all for its power on any allusion to a novel written twenty years earlier, or on any experience at all of its author's other work. It is magnificently self-sufficient, relying on what Beckett has accurately called 'the power of the text to claw'. It is an astonishing achievement; even the banalities fall with horrible weight. But characteristically, achieving what it does, it makes use time and again of elements the author has employed before: the chess game, the man in the chair, the man telling himself a lifetime story, the master and servant equivocally related, the ritual cruelty on which no one comments because no one expects better, the splendidly shaped sentences, the silences. The commonest direction is (*Pause*), and the actors had better be virtuosi of the unspoken. The reader of the Beckett canon can of course notice contrasts and developments inaccessible to the audience who are present only for this one performance of this one work. The same is true of all Beckett's plays. It is also true that such a reader may be misled, especially when, as in the late short works, the ones that follow *Endgame*, the very small number of elements in use enforces his recognition that he has met them before. He may easily suppose that Beckett simply writes and rewrites the same work, which is not the case. Beckett plays quite different games with the same pieces. To stress the similarities may enlighten, but similarities must be noted with caution, lest we place ourselves in the position of supposing that having seen one chess game—rooks, kings, bishops, pawns—we have seen them all. Each Beckett project starts afresh, a new work, a new kind of work, a new kind of experience. There is always attrition, as there always is in chess. There is always a mate, or the nearing threat of a mate. But no two games are the same.

10   Krapp's Last Tape

Beckett described *Krapp's Last Tape*, about the time he was finishing it, as a play for one actor; he did not mention the tape recorder. When he wrote the play, as a matter of fact, he had never seen a recorder. The rumour, however, was sufficient: a machine anyone might possess, which could store away for future decantation whatever story one chose to tell in its presence, every pause, every nuance, every intonation inflexibly, irrevocably registered: more faithful than any memory, yet implacable and hence insensitive as memory is not. Since home tape recording began in the middle 1950s, and since Krapp's archive spans more than thirty years of tapes, the time of the play is put forward to 'a late evening in the future'. It feels, however, like any Beckettian present.

The place is 'Krapp's den'. Krapp ('White face. Purple nose. Disordered grey hair.') is the familiar clown. His trousers are too short for him, he sports a 'surprising pair of dirty white boots, size ten at least, very narrow and pointed.' He sighs, fumbles, squints at keys and written papers, extracts bananas from a desk drawer kept resolutely locked, skids on banana peels, stares vacuously before him with a banana end in his mouth. It should be clear that we are to expect 'characterization' neither from author nor from actor, beyond the clown stereotype, and the purpose of the opening business would seem to be to establish that point. It is against this lay figure, refugee from some vaudeville, that the rhetoric of passion is going to play, and out of the heart of the machine.

The great ledger, when he searches its pages, yields a filing entry: 'Box . . . three . . . spool . . . five'. The word 'spool' delights him: ' "Spooool!" (*Happy smile*).' He reads the ledger summary of box three, spool five: 'Mother at rest at last' and 'slight improvement in bowel condition' are nearly adjacent entries. Was that juxtaposition entered by a sardonic hand, or is it merely the convention of itemization that levels great things beside small, death and constipation? (Readers of *Mercier et Camier* may remember the chapter résumés, intercalated with a comparably impartial detachment.) There is a puzzling entry: 'Memorable equinox'. It puzzles Krapp, who, however memorable it was, apparently no longer remembers it. And another entry is interrupted by the turning page: 'Farewell to—(*he turns the page*)—love'. Here, if the actor turns the page expressively, the word 'love' will become as flat as 'bowel condition'.

When he switches on the machine, box three, spool five pours into today's air the voice of a much earlier Krapp, it is clear: strong and rather pompous, the author's direction says, the voice of a man on his thirty-ninth birthday, a solitary already, constipated, addicted to bananas (essentials do not change), and fresh, then, from listening to the tape of a still earlier Krapp. 'Hard to believe I was ever that young whelp,' says Krapp-39. 'The voice! Jesus! And the aspirations! . . . And the resolutions!' That still earlier Krapp, the Krapp of say twenty-eight, had startled himself by his statistics on his own drinking ('Seventeen hundred hours, out of the preceding eight thousand odd, consumed on licensed premises alone. More than twenty percent, say forty percent of his waking life').[11] He had also made 'Plans for a less . . . (*hesitates*) . . . engrossing sexual life': and had sneered at an even earlier Krapp, the Krapp of 'his youth'. Now Krapp-39 in turn sneers at Krapp-28, while Krapp-69 listens.

Krapp-69 still drinks too much, but apparently in solitude, not on licensed premises; and is still constipated, still has the addiction to bananas Krapp-39 had reprobated. We shall learn that his sexual life is no longer 'engrossing', but that seems not to be a consequence of plans and resolutions. It has rather to do with age, and with his habit of communing with a machine.

Here Alec Reid's description cannot be bettered:

As we listen, we become aware . . . of three distinct sound-patterns. Gradually we distinguish an even-paced measure for narrative speech, a slower, long-drawn-out lyrical tempo, and a brisker, harsh, sardonic tone, and we notice the periods of silence marking the change from one rhythm to the next. From the interplay of these rhythms we gradually realize that Krapp-at-39 is torn by two radically opposed elements in his character, and that the conflict still racks the old man sitting at the table in front of us.[12]

That is accurately observed, and it is also accurate to observe that the author has written these rhythms into the speeches, and not left them to the insight of the actor. Mr Reid's example, Krapp-39's account of the November day when his mother died, illustrates it well. It illustrates one more thing, Krapp's habit of detachment. He sat outside by the canal watching her window, 'wishing she were gone' (the wish fathered by compassion? impatience? boredom?) and recalling this, Krapp-39 used the pedantic word, 'viduity': 'lay a-dying, in the late autumn, after her long viduity'. Krapp-69 can no longer remember the meaning of the word 'viduity' and stops the machine to look it up. Krapp-39 had used that word, and words like it, with a certain self-appreciating pedantry for which Krapp-69 can no longer command the attention, though he cannot forego the research.

Krapp-39, then, sitting by the canal, saw the blind in his mother's room go down ('one of those dirty brown roller affairs'). He was 'throwing a ball for a little white dog, as chance would have it'.

I happened to look up and there it was. All over and done with, at last. I sat on for a few moments with the ball in my hand and the dog yelping and pawing at me. (*Pause*.) Moments. Her moments. My moments. (*Pause*.) The dog's moments. (*Pause*.) In the end I held it out to him and he took it in his mouth, gently, gently. A small, old, black, hard, solid rubber ball. (*Pause*.) I shall feel it, in my hand, until

my dying day. (*Pause*.) I might have kept it. (*Pause*.) But I gave it
to the dog. (*Pause*.) Ah well. . . .

There are the two rhythms: the lingering lyricism—

Moments. Her moments. My moments.

and the sardonic interjection—

The dog's moments.

And the pity is self-pity: 'I shall feel it, in my hand, until my
dying day. (*Pause*.) I might have kept it. (*Pause*.) But I gave
it to the dog.'

A man who withheld himself; a man who recalls the dying
day of his mother with less feeling than he evokes in himself
with the phrase about his own 'dying day', the day up to which
the feel of the little black ball will be memorable. (And when
Krapp-69 read 'black ball' in the ledger he was puzzled.) A
man, moreover, who had a vision into the heart of things,
that is, into himself, on a 'memorable equinox'. Krapp-69
cannot be bothered to rehear the account of this vision, pregnant
though it was with promise of great works now (at sixty-nine)
not achieved and not achievable. We hear the account in
snatches, notably the fragment, 'clear to me at last that the
dark I have always struggled to keep under is in reality my
most—'. A man struggling to keep the dark under, that is
how Krapp-39 saw himself: a man who should rather draw
on it, as on a capital asset. It seemed a revelation.[13] Cursing
at this pretentious nonsense Krapp-69 jerks the tape forward,
and lights by chance in the midst of Krapp-39's 'farewell to
love'. A lyrical cadence catches his ear:

. . . my face in her breasts and my hand on her. We lay there without
moving. But under us all moved, and moved us, gently, up and down,
and from side to side.

He winds this back and replays it in its context: a stream of
marvellous sensuous detail, exquisitely cadenced: he and she
in a punt, drifting, engaged in a last amour before agreeing

that it is no good going on; she facing up toward the bright sky, 'the eyes just slits, because of the glare. I bent over her to get them in the shadow and they opened.' 'The eyes', he says, not 'her eyes', and goes on to recall how he exploited a reflex, for he is recording this after renouncing her, and renouncing love, and it is sustaining to characterize things clinically. But the clinical is swept away.

(*Pause. Low.*) Let me in. (*Pause.*) We drifted in among the flags and stuck. The way they went down, sighing, before the stem! (*Pause.*) I lay down across her with my face in her breasts and my hand on her. We lay there without moving. But under us all moved, and moved us, gently, up and down, and from side to side.

Krapp-69, an elderly half-impotent drunk, savours this wonder, broods, drinks, records a savage reply concerning his state at sixty-nine, rips it off the machine, and replays once more the farewell to love: '. . . but under us all moved, and moved us, gently, up and down, and from side to side.' And this last time he lets Krapp-39's postscript be played out: ' . . . Perhaps my best years are gone. When there was a chance of happiness. But I wouldn't want them back. Not with the fire in me now. No, I wouldn't want them back.'

No, he had bidden love farewell, and the human world farewell, and big with insight concerning the dark inside him had embarked, apparently, on his *magnum opus*. ('Seventeen copies sold,' records Krapp-69, 'of which eleven at trade price to free circulating libraries beyond the seas. Getting known.') Would he not have done better not to shut his heart? The fire in him—the fire of 39—has guttered to the embers we see. What is there left? Again to replay that tape: the last love, the magical cadences, reduced to a canned voice, a figure or two of rhetoric, a rhythm, sure to exhaust its effect with repetition because it is a voice from the far side of death.

Always this gentlest, most courteous of writers probes personae who have made the Great Refusal. Always the hinge on which swings the door to shut them into their ashen world is love, the withholding of love, the rejection of the claims of

affection, of others. Krapp is a lesser Hamm, passive before
the tapes which correspond to Hamm's effort at going on with
his story: a Hamm devoid of gusto and panache, no tragic
actor but a circus clown, with no one to tyrannize over and
no energy, one surmises, for tyrannizing, drinking and shuffling and gorging himself on bananas, picking his past snatch
by snatch from a ledger. It is a hell, or perhaps a purgatory
without promise of issue. No, not a purgatory; a purgatory
without issue is a Protestant hell.

For Beckett's work draws on two spiritual traditions by
which history has shaped the specifically Protestant character:
the personal testimony, and the issueless confrontation with
conscience. We may think of them as combined, and as constituting a confession without absolution or hope of absolution,
because no man can absolve, and touch with God has either
been lost or not initiated. When the Reformers abandoned
the sacramental universe (which, reinforced by scholasticism,
underwrote a Joyce's rigorous externality, persisting beyond
Joyce's loss of belief), and when Faith, not Works, and Faith
moreover attested to by an Experience, became the note of
salvation, then the literature of reformed Christianity became
narrative, confessional, and entoiled in the retracing of conscience, or else with testimony to the all-important Experience.
These are by no means exclusively Protestant categories, but
we may still usefully say that Beckett's visions of endlessness
—the men who wait and wait, the minds that re-enact and re-
enact, the people locked by memories of choices once taken,
powerless unless some power choose to act upon them——correspond to a habit of mind that since the seventeenth century
has received a specific religious shaping, so that Beckett's
Protestant upbringing is perceptible in the midst of the agnos-
ticism into which he passed without, he says, any crisis.

Krapp-39 recorded, as he supposed, a moment of insight
which was like a moment of conversion: he had seen light,
he said, in coming to appreciate his inner dark. 'My dissolution of storm and night', runs one of the sentences we are
prevented from hearing totally, 'with the light of the under-

standing and the fire—' That fire, surely, is 'the fire in me now' on which the Krapp-39 tape ends by dwelling with satisfaction. Instead, as he can judge after thirty more years, he had recorded the moment when he shut himself off from light and from warmth, and there is no recovering these.

The Beckett books and plays are repeatedly public confessions by men who have cut themselves off and have nothing left but the language to fondle, old language, new language. Keeping going, that's their job now.

11 How It Is

In 1958 Beckett said that he did not see how he could possibly write another novel. *The Unnamable* was an impasse, the *Texts for Nothing* were unavailing efforts to break out of it, and *From an Abandoned Work* had been abandoned. The following year he began what was published in French (1961) as *Comment c'est* and in English (1964) as *How It Is*. We may as well call it a novel. It presents with agonizing explicitness a system of interpersonal relationships which seemed to most reviewers not to describe the way it is at all. Yet it reflects—there's no denying this—the way it was when it was getting written; the effort to get it written is candidly there on the page, a major theme.

One aspect of this effort is that the book nowhere achieves so much as a sentence. Unpunctuated murmurs are spaced down the page:

how it was I quote before Pim with Pim after Pim how it is three parts I say it as I hear it

voice once without quaqua on all sides then in me when the panting stops tell me again finish telling me invocation [...]

my life last state last version ill-said ill-heard ill-recaptured ill-murmured in the mud brief movements of the lower face losses everywhere

There are three parts, and of virtually equal length; and the timemarkers, before Pim, with Pim, after Pim, correspond exactly to the content of the three parts. The panting, the sense of indescribable labour, are sustained to the end, and the last words are:

good good end at last of part three and last that's how it was end of
quotation after Pim how it is

We should note that this is something new for a Beckett
protagonist, this heroic completion of a plan announced
beforehand. Malone planned out cozily what he meant to
write, Present State, Stories, Inventory of Possessions, and
botched all of it in his panic and confusion. Krapp sat down
to record his reflections on his sixty-ninth year, and ended
up ripping the tape from the machine and hurling it across
the room. Whether The Unnamable executed what he meant
to or not, beyond keeping going, it is hard to say, so tenuous
in the nature of the case are his proposals. But the man in
How It Is, if he cannot say what Dr Johnson said of the *Dictionary*, that he understood very well what had to be done,
and very well how to do it, and did it very well, can say at least
that what he proposed he completed: for what that may be
worth, since it fell into ruins as he was completing it.

It fell into ruins for the highly Beckettian reason that logic
tangled an apparently simple idea in more and more supposititious detail, which grew as the Lynch family grew in the mind
of Watt until the mental edifice was overwhelmed. He is left
with the bleak triumph of having traversed his schema to the
end, come what come might. It is as though a man had laboured all his life to establish a mathematical theorem of which,
on his deathbed, he succeeded in proving the falsity, though
the analogy fails in this particular, that he cannot even be
sure there is such a thing as a deathbed. He feels sure at the
end of one thing only, that he lies flat on his belly in mud, in
darkness, his arms spread cruciform. This too may not be
certain, but the 'voice' seems to endorse it, doubtful though
the existence of the voice may be.

The scheme had entailed the existence of other people:
of Pim, first of all, toward whom for many pages the narrative
dragged its agonizing way. Unlike Godot, on whose whims
we wait, Pim is a goal toward which (toward whom?) we travel.
We travel in the dark, extended in mud, dragging a sack of
tinned fish and a tin-opener. And there was—a theme common

to many Beckett works—a life before this one, of which glimpses descend, memories, unbidden, often bitter. That life was 'up there in the light', and this life, down here in the dark, differs from the eternal life of Dante's damned chiefly in its vagueness, for Dante's damned when Dante questions them can explain smartly what law they transgressed.

I mention Dante because one point of departure for the book may have been *Inferno* VII, where the souls of the Sullen ('the Gloomy-sluggish' in the Temple edition) lie immersed in mud, and gurgle a statement of the case in their throats since the mud prevents their speaking or singing plainly. Sullenness, that is a sin to catch Beckett's attention. A sullen man would be like a corrosive Belacqua. And earlier in the same Canto Dante displays a tribe who move perpetually back and forth along a semi-circle, banging each other, cursing, about-facing. This may have contributed to the vision of the endless procession of tormentors and tormented in the third part of *How It Is*, though the special logistics of Beckett's formulation are his own.

It seems relevant also to mention that we are perhaps some way down a serial hell, in which the same soul may undergo successive lives. For the nameless protagonist mentions things that don't seem to be allotted him 'this time'. For instance:

no the wish to be less wretched a little the wish for a little beauty no when the panting stops I hear nothing of the kind that's not how I'm told this time

In such dim allusions to yet earlier lives which are earlier tellings we have the usual cunning doubling: a Beckett character recalling the days when he lived Murphy's life or Molloy's, and a soul in a hell where you remember previous hells, fleetingly. We should not think of this as a trick, any more than the references in *Endgame* or *Happy Days* to the fact that we watch actors trapped in a play. It is of a piece with Beckett's peculiar candour, which will extrapolate fiction only from accessible fact, and always ground the illusion of the moment on the moment's immediacy, in this case on the fact that one more Beckett character, a new mutation of the previous Beckett characters, is making his way through a fiction that is costing unprecedented effort.

life then without callers present formulation no callers this time no stories but mine no silence but the silence I must break when I can bear it no more it's with that I have to last

And these gobbets of utterance are paced and cadenced like elegiac *vers libre*, though the reader, sharing the protagonist's vigil, must detect for himself the boundaries of the phrases and reconstitute the muted *bel canto*:

life then without callers
                present formulation
no callers this time
no stories but mine
no silence
     but the silence
             I must break
             when I can bear it no more
it's with that I have to last

No callers, but some ancient vignettes. He remembers praying at his mother's knee:

the huge head hatted with birds and flowers is bowed down over my curls the eyes burn with severe love I offer her mine pale upcast to the sky whence cometh our help and which I know perhaps even then with time shall pass away

in a word bolt upright on a cushion my knees whelmed in a night-shirt I pray according to her instructions

that's not all she closes her eyes and drones a snatch of the so-called Apostles' Creed I steal a look at her lips

she stops her eyes burn down on me again I cast up mine in haste and repeat awry

the air thrills with the hum of insects

that's all it goes out like a lamp blown out

Though unpunctuated these are formal sentences, the book's convention for such memories. Moreover Beckett has allowed to be reproduced at least twice—in *Beckett at Sixty*, opposite page 24, and in *Beckett par lui-même*, page 6—the earliest known photograph of himself, kneeling 'whelmed in a night-shirt' on a cushion at the knee of his extravagantly hatted mother. The candour is disarming with which we are enabled to discern that the bleak novel draws on actual memories.

And if the character has some of the author's memories, the character has also a strange consciousness of the author bent over his worktable:

he lives bent over me that's the life he has been given all my visible surface bathing in the light of his lamps when I go he follows me bent in two

This gives one kind of explanation for 'I say it as I hear it', since the words I say are drawn from the author's brain. It helps us understand too the ambiguous time, in which the present of part one, my journey toward Pim, is also the past, while the future, part three, to which I have not yet attained, is How It Is; for the moment of writing is always now, and yet the author when he begins has thought out the end, and the last pages (unwritten) occupy the vantage-point (How It Is) from which the first are undertaken. Simple practical facts of authorship, and they permit a shuffling of times that allows us to intuit the feel of eternity.

And the man who crawls through this dark eternity is the familar loveless Beckett protagonist. 'Above in the light', we gather, in that other life, he was loveless. Things merely happened. There was the remembered scene with the girl:

suddenly we are eating sandwiches alternate bites I mine she hers and exchanging endearments my sweet girl I bite she swallows my sweet boy she bites I swallow we don't yet coo with our bills full

and there is the bleak self-appraisal—

... understood everything and forgave nothing never could never disapproved anything really not even cruelty to animals never loved anything

And now he is drawn toward Pim by a promise of fellowship;

and after agonies of zigzag progress, the hand stretched forward to claw the mud for a new heave touches 'instead of the
familiar slime an arse': Pim.

And in part two ('Happy time in its way') we learn of the
time with Pim.

in the dark the mud my head against his my side glued to his my right
arm round his shoulders his cries have ceased we lie thus a good moment they are good moments

But on, to the training of Pim, who is taught by a cruel be-
haviourist regimen[14] to sing, to stop, to speak, to speak louder,
at the application of savage stimuli, including the blade of
the can-opener. This is done by tormenting him till he gives
the correct response, which he knows is correct because a
bang on the skull does not reprove it. Eventually seven se-
parate torments control seven responses, a considerable repertory under the circumstances. It is the only way ('I am
not a brute as I may have said', and 'with someone to keep
me company I would have been a different man more universal'). And since I have no speech, I impart myself to Pim by
writing on his back with my nails, 'from left to right and top
to bottom as in our civilization'. He imparts to Pim what is
closest to his heart, the particulars of his long-lost faith, 'the
lamb black with the world's sins the world cleansed the three
persons [. . .] and that belief said to have been mine the feeling since then vast stretch of time that I'd find it again the blue
cloak the pigeon the miracles he understood'; or no, he imparted
none of this to Pim, rather, he says, he got Pim to impart Pim's
life to him:

that life then said to have been his invented remembered a little of
each no knowing that thing above he gave it to me I made it mine

And Pim got that life from someone else before, and I shall
transmit it to someone else later on; for there are beginning
to be premonitions of a day when I shall lie like Pim, and a
certain Bom, with sack and can-opener, will come rudely to
me and serve me as I serve Pim now. And a single life-story
will   be   transmitted,   passed   along   the   unending   series,

modified by each in accordance with his preferences and needs. For all men have needs and preferences, and all men (here) have the one life.

That life had a deathbed, in a hospital ('Pam Prim . . . dying forgiving all white'), and papa's death too, and mama and her bible ('man his days as grass flower of the field wind above in the clouds'[15]) and myself always on the move, 'never anyone never knew anyone always ran fled elsewhere some other place my life above places paths nothing else'. The death of Pam Prim oppresses him; she jumped or fell from a window after their love had faded, and asked for a little green—holly or berries, he says in his first version, mistletoe in his second— to relieve the hospital white; and he had lied about not being able to find any, lied very circumstantially, describing a search. This is Pim's life? Mine?

. . . he can't give any more me permitting or thump on skull I can't take any more it's one or the other and what then him me I'll ask him but first me when Pim stops what becomes of me . . .

Anyhow 'the voice stops for one or the other reason and life along with it above in the light and we along with it that is what becomes of us'.

Why do we like to hear other people talk? In this cruel place where we care nothing for them, it is because they tell us our own story, and no Beckett protagonist can do without his story being told him, by himself or by another.

On to part three, and early on there are memories, if memories is what they are, of a time before part one, a time like part two except that I played Pim's part and a certain Bem played mine. (Observe the pattern of these names. What is 'my' name? Can it be Sam?) Then from having been Bem's victim I crawled on to become Pim's tormentor. Now I lie awaiting my turn to be Bom's victim. This is our opportunity to observe that the whole sequence is elaborated from a curious little work called *Act Without Words II*, which was published in 1959, the year in which *Comment c'est* was begun. Two sacks stand at the right of the stage. Enter, from the wings, a goad,

which jabs the nearest sack until a slow morose man gets out
of it, does his weary day's ritual with prayers, pills and food,
then carries both sacks to stage centre, exchanging their order
as he sets them down. Last of all he crawls back into his empty
sack. The goad, now equipped with a wheel to steady its aim,
glides in like a billiard cue and jabs once more, at the other
sack this time, and a brisk busy man gets out, performs very
rapidly an intricate busy day's ritual (brushing teeth, combing
hair, brushing clothes, consulting watch and map and compass),
then carries both sacks all the way to the left of the stage. Once
more they are interchanged, and the goad, on two wheels this
time, jabs till the slow man emerges from his sack . . . . An
infinite ritual, clearly, on an endless rectilinear track; one
supposes that the proprietors of the goad keep an infinity of
wheels. And the men, a kind of Molloy, a kind of Moran,
live out their alternating days perhaps in unawareness of one
another's existence.

The sacks in *How It Is* are not inhabited but dragged, and
the men, far from hoisting one another like luggage, crawl
between one another, alternately moving and stationary, to
enact the alternate roles of tormentor and victim. The central
metaphor is retained, life as an endless track where people
are as objects to other people, but the dreadful rite with the
can-opener is suffused with efforts to make them more than
objects, to enact a ritual of companionship at once cruel and
tender. And they seem to be serial selves, and it all seems to
be one life. Between the two works there is another difference,
more pertinent. *Act Without Words II*, being a mime, is utterly explicit as to the empirical facts, though tacit as to their
possible meaning. How the sacks are moved, for instance,
we cannot doubt, nor with what equivalence of intervals between
station-points, and with what symmetry of transposition.
And the principle which initiates each tick of this cycle is un-
ambiguous too: it is the goad. What the protagonists make
of it all we cannot guess, nor even whether they give it any
thought, or are aware that they are not alone. On the other
hand *How It Is*, being yet one more whirl of the wordy-gurdy,

is told from within, from the dark, and is tirelessly explicit about the feelings that pervade this universe, so far as they can be defined. It is vague however about the logistic arrangements, as vague as one private would be, on a muddy night, about the battle-plan in which he is a pawn. Impulsions, intervals, directions, chronologies, are utterly obscure and subjects for anxious conjecture. What is pervasive is the ache for others; the ache may even conjure up the others, such others as Pim and Bem and Bom. They are needed, therefore they must be; and it is curious what difficulty we have distinguishing 'my' life from Pim's.

Now, in part three, as he lies after Pim's departure, the symmetries, the ordonnances, the order of things on which *Act Without Words II* concentrated the audience's attention, begin to occupy his mind. That he left Bem to reach Pim, that he awaits Bom Pim having left, that Pim in his turn crawls toward a new rendezvous, such symmetries preoccupy and soothe, for however miserable the goings-on make you, it is soothing to have an overview of what is going on. He devises his overview under fearful pressure, like a theologian obsessed with suffering and determined to grasp the Divine Mercy's scheme. And the overview wavers: 'very pretty but not right somehow something wrong something quite wrong'.

It's the sack. My sack burst just before I came to Pim. Then Pim left his sack with me. And if everyone leaves his sack, how does he come to be dragging a sack as he crawls? 'That sack without which no journey'?

He abandons this problem, not having solved it but patched it with a hypothesis of sacks found on the way ('I must have found it there's reason in me yet'). Next, the question of number. Are there perhaps just three of us? Four? A million? Are we to conceive that 'nameless each awaits his Bom nameless goes towards his Pim'? It grows clear (clear?) that however populous this darkness, I have to do only with Bom and Pim. (The unit of experience, by the way, is then like a French Resistance cell; I am to know only my two neighbours. And a member of Beckett's cell 'sang' under torture.)

alone murmur of millions and of three our journeys couples and abandons and the name we give to one another and give and give again

All this is as difficult to follow as it is difficult for the protagonist to keep straight, and the reader shares his uncertainties, his efforts and mental agonies.

He works out a neat scheme entailing four of us, does calculations entailing a million of us, discovers a flaw in any finite number, and concludes that either 'I am alone and no further problem or else we are innumerable and no further problem either'; no problem, that is,

save that of conceiving but no doubt it can be done a procession in a straight line with neither head nor tail in the dark the mud with all the various infinitudes that such a conception involves

The other alternative grows increasingly attractive: that 'I' am alone, and that the voice in response to which 'I say it as I hear it' is filling me with illusion. There is more about the voice, the voices; then the sacks begin to worry him again.

For if the sacks lie in wait for us to find them, then on our journeyings we must scale, each of us, a mountain of sacks:

such an acervation of sacks at the very outset that all progress impossible and no sooner imparted to the caravan the unthinkable first impulsion than arrested for ever and frozen in injustice

How they multiply like the Lynch family, all those sacks! But scanning the spectacle of immobilized beings interposed between mountains of provisions, he does not dwell on its humour but on its injustice. So they cannot, the sacks, have been present like us from the outset, and we must postulate a providence: 'an intelligence somewhere a love who all along the track at the right places according as we need them deposits our sacks'. This being moreover (with 'exceptional powers or else at his beck assistants innumerable') must lend the ear which receives our murmurings ('otherwise desert flower'), exercising therefore 'that strange care for us not to be found among us', and to this being must be imputed the voice which speaks through us all. He is therefore listening to himself, imperfectly recounted. For various reasons he seems unthinkable.

Other worlds are nonetheless thinkable, 'as just as ours but less exquisitely organized'; and coming near the most exposed of nerves, a ghastly parody is generated of the heaven where there is no marrying nor giving in marriage:

one perhaps there is one perhaps somewhere merciful enough to shelter such frolics where no one ever abandons anyone and no one ever waits for anyone and never two bodies touch

And as for the possibility of an arrangement like the present one being sustained without sacks of food, we are invited to consider:

that for the likes of us and no matter how we are recounted there is more nourishment in a cry nay a sigh torn from one whose only good is silence or in speech extorted from one at last delivered from its use than sardines can ever offer

. . . which is to say, in consonance if not compliance with Matthew IV: 4, that in another world they do not live by sardines alone, but by every word that proceeds from the mouth of Pim.

Whereupon suddenly the whole thing is swept away. It is simplest to suppose that he is alone, that there was no Pim, no sack, no procession, nay, no movement; that he lies in the mud, spreadeagled, and may think of dying, but not with confidence. In sweeping it all away he sweeps the author away too, the being in another world 'whose kind of dream I am'. An immobile thought, then, without a thinker; and if it is from the voices that he obtains confirmation of this, he must assume that the voices are his own.

Which is How It Is, that we don't know how it is, but know, or maybe imagine, three agonies: of the journey, of the coupling, of thought; Beckett's Inferno, told from the inside, not like Dante's from the standpoint of a privileged tourist, and in its starkness, uncertainty, and paradoxical intelligibility a very twentieth-century hell.

12 Happy Days

Winnie chattering away, forcing herself through the formulae of cheerful utterance, keeping going, just keeping going, making the day's project out of being happy; Willie grunting, slouching, ignoring her except when much solicited: a day, shall we say, in a shabby-genteel flat where they work hard at being cheerful. It's a curiously *English* play, English in Winnie's tacit assumption that one has a duty not to lapse into gloom; English in the endless struggle to devalue little annoyances, to cherish small mercies; English in the intent façade of garrulity. This is not to say that women everywhere—people everywhere—do not recognize an obligation not to despair. But the unquestioning assumption that the warp and woof of an unfulfilling day consist in maintaining one's cheer is a premise of English gentility as perhaps of no other. Anyone who suspects that Beckett's way of writing is simply to project his own moods should study his portrait of Winnie—no doubt drawn from memories of his London years, a quarter-century before he wrote the play. And the author's affection for Winnie is surely explicit; she is given every opportunity—granted the limited facilities—to be endearing. The actress moreover is given a hundred chances to show what a voice can do, with caresses of inflection, to transform simple words into poetry. Of her parasol:

I suppose I might—(*takes up parasol*)—yes, I suppose I might . . . hoist this thing now. (*Begins to unfurl it. Following punctuated by mechanical difficulties overcome.*) One keeps putting off—putting up—for fear of putting up—too soon—and the day goes by—quite by—without one's having put up—at all. (*Parasol now fully open. Turned to her right she*

twirls it idly this way and that.) Ah yes, so little to say, so little to do, and
the fear so great, certain days, of finding oneself . . . left, with hours still
to run, before the bell for sleep, and nothing more to say, nothing more
to do, that the days go by, certain days go by, quite by, the bell goes,
and little or nothing said, little or nothing done. (*Raising parasol.*)
That is the danger. (*Turning front.*) To be guarded against. (*She
gazes front, holding up parasol with right hand. Maximum pause.*)

Of words, and of small duties:

Is not that so, Willie, that even words fail, at times? (*Pause. Back front.*)
What is one to do then, until they come again? Brush and comb the
hair, if it has not been done, or if there is some doubt, trim the nails
if they are in need of trimming, these things tide one over. (*Pause.*)
That is what I mean. (*Pause.*) That is all I mean. (*Pause.*) That is
what I find so wonderful, that not a day goes by—(*smile*)—to speak
in the old style—(*smile off*) without some blessing—(WILLIE *collapses
behind slope, his head disappears,* WINNIE *turns towards event*)—in
disguise.

Of Willie's incompetent locomotion:

Not the crawler you were, poor darling. (*Pause.*) No, not the crawler
I gave my heart to. (*Pause.*) The hands and knees, love, try the hands
and knees. (*Pause.*) The knees! The knees! (*Pause.*) What a curse,
mobility!

It's a splendid virtuoso part, though an immobilized one like
Hamm's, and her simple love, largely unrequited, for Willie,
lifts the tedium to crescendos of chirpy pathos.

All but the crawling-speech, these speeches might be spoken
in any flat on the Edgware Road. But of course they are spoken
under conditions never explained, simply taken for granted
as so many inconveniences—cockroaches, for instance, defective plumbing, damp, dry rot—are taken for granted. The
present condition would appear to be that the earth's rotation has
become very slow, hence the days very long and very hot. To
speak of days at all is 'to speak in the old style'; she cannot
break the habit, but never fails to observe its incongruity.
And the earth seems nearly depopulated, though a couple
did once come strolling by, she remembers them. And the

heat increases. Her parasol, in the play's most spectacular
event, takes fire by spontaneous combustion, and she wonders
if she herself will not melt in the end, 'Oh, I do not mean necessarily burst into flames, no, just little by little be charred
to a black cinder, all this—(*ample gesture of arms*)—visible
flesh.' It is as though the flash of a Hydrogen Bomb and its
power to incinerate were being lived through in excruciating
slow motion.

Or not quite, since we are (as always) on stage, and the first
sound is the prompter's bell, and almost her first words—
'Begin, Winnie'—are like the words of an actress steeling
herself to play the part one more time. (It is an uncomfortable
role, we are to reflect, and night after night the woman before
us must go through with it, under fierce unchanging artificial
lights.) Tomorrow, she reflects, there will be another parasol
to put up (though it, too, will burn), and tomorrow the little
mirror she breaks on a stone (she breaks it merely to enforce
this point) will be intact again in her bag, if the property-master
is not negligent. It is a curious effect, the hidden functionaries
of the theatre who check the contents of bags and arrange com-
bustible umbrellas being transformed, by a few words, into
presiding powers, workers of mysterious miracles; merciful
miracles since resources are replenished, merciless since no
headway is made, not even headway toward some abyss. Beckett has invoked the repeatability of the play before, the plight
of actors trapped in parts, but never so deftly, never with such
buoyant pathos. *Happy Days* is like a companion-piece to
Endgame, with cheer where the latter flaunted cruelty, and
renewability where the latter suffered attrition. All the world's
a stage, all the world's a Woolworth's; there are always more
parasols, more looking-glasses, more words.

For the words are properties also. As parasols are fetched
from shops, so words from poets, and it is surprising what
resources the poets afford, for cheering one up in the face of
the irremediable. 'Fear no more the heat o' the sun', she quotes
at one point, when Willie has crawled into the shade; and
'Hail, holy light', as her eyes open on yet another blinding

prospect, and as she finishes making up her lips, words Romeo spoke over the inanimate Juliet flit through her head:

> Thou art not conquer'd; beauty's ensign yet
> Is crimson in thy lips and in thy cheeks
> And death's pale flag is not advancèd there.

Winnie's ensign of beauty comes from a tube, and Romeo has his back to her, absorbed in a newspaper, and it is she who speaks, not he, so the scene has to be somewhat transposed:

> (. . . *She pulls down spectacles and resumes lips.* WILLIE *opens newspaper, hands invisible. Tops of yellow sheets appear on either side of his head.* WINNIE *finishes lips, inspects them in mirror held a little further away.*) Ensign crimson. (WILLIE *turns page.* WINNIE *lays down lipstick and mirror, turns towards bag.*) Pale flag.

One enhances one's experience with words one would have been unqualified to compose, and has for an instant a taste of human grandeur. This is a service writers perform for us, a service less attended to than it might be in schools where the didactic functions of literature nourish the self-esteem of teachers. Poets give us words to say, though they may be imperfectly remembered when we have occasion to say them.

What are those exquisite lines? (*Pause.*) Go forget me why should something o'er that something shadow fling . . . go forget me . . . why should sorrow . . . brightly smile . . . go forget me . . . never hear me . . . sweetly smile . . .brightly sing . . .(*Pause. With a sigh.*) One loses one's classics. (*Pause.*) Oh not all. (*Pause.*) A part. (*Pause.*) A part remains. (*Pause.*) That is what I find so wonderful, a part remains, of one's classics, to help one through the day.

Quotations abound; an inventory would be pointless. For that matter most of the play (of any play) is quotation, quotation from that eponymous poet the Folk, who have shaped the idiom of which each Winnie at need avails herself.

The whole day has flown—(*smile, smile off*)—flown by, quite by, and no song of any class, kind or description. (*Pause.*) There is a problem here. (*Pause*.) One cannot sing . . . just like that, no. (*Pause*.) It bubbles up, for some unknown reason, the time is ill chosen, one chokes it back. (*Pause*.) One says, Now is the time, it is now or never, and one cannot. (*Pause*.) Simply cannot sing. (*Pause*.) Not a note.

'Just like that'; 'for some unknown reason'; 'the time is ill chosen'; 'not a note'. Not a phrase in this speech but is like these, familiar idiom, shaped by the imagination of the race, validated (like the familiar quotations in Bartlett) by collective usage. That is Winnie's resource, ultimately, the human community, available to her in speech, its legacy of speech, though hardly a soul any longer comes this way.

And she sinks; we all do. In the first act she can rummage (like Malone) through her possessions. In the second she can only look toward them but not finger them, having sunk further, in fact up to the neck. This is unexplained. There was a day when she 'was not yet caught—in this way'—and had the use of her legs; there was the day of the first kiss, the first ball, the day Willie proposed ('I worship you, Winnie, be mine. Life's a mockery without Win.') She is caught now, that is all. It is no more explained than would be an incurable disease. Willie is caught too, not in a quagmire, but in a defect of locomotion that compels him to get about only on all fours. (Locomotion, for most Beckett characters, is so peculiar that we are seldom surprised when one of them is deprived of it.) He might crawl away, but he does not, which is a comfort, and perhaps a mute fidelity, unless it bespeaks a lacuna in his imagination. And when he crawls round at the end, and up her mound, and gazes into her eyes, or maybe glares ('Don't look at me like that! Have you gone out of your head, Willie? Out of your poor old wits, Willie?') it is an open question whether he is moved to reanimate the past, or has simply made up his mind to use the revolver that lies conspicuous before her on the mound. It may even be his intention to use it on her; his tastes are sedentary, his devotion is to the obituaries and the advertisements in *Reynolds' News*, and her talk, talk, talk, it may be, has driven him mad.

Valiant, spunky, imprisoned in habit and in routine, she

lives without letting herself know it in a world of little love, and puts amorous construction—to the extent of singing the Merry Widow Waltz—on what for all we know may be a murderous glare. The play, an emptiness filled by indomitable energy, is Beckett's ambiguous celebration of human persistence, which has at many times made it unfashionable to reflect, with Dr Johnson, that there is much in human life to be endured, and little to be enjoyed.

13 Play

Winnie, trapped, is curiously free. In *Play*, Beckett's ultimate version of the Protestant Hell, everyone is trapped in a condemnation to repeat, repeat, versions of what happened elsewhere, long ago, not to their credit. They are being interrogated, and speak only when solicited, but the interrogation is absent-minded and often abandons them in mid-narrative, sometimes in mid-sentence. There is no sign that the interrogator is *listening*, let alone paying attention. In fact it is simply a spotlight, swivelling at whim from face to face, in a random order. ('Mere eye, no mind,' says the man.) A speech commences when the spotlight strikes a face, but not immediately: only after a delay of about one second, during which an effort occurs which one of the women likens to 'dragging a great roller, on a scorching day. The strain . . . to get it moving, momentum coming—kill it and strain again.' So the stopping and starting is as much a part of their agony as the speaking. The light is an agony too, and the 'endurable moments' are 'When you go out—and I go out.' There is even hope, of a sort ('Some day you will tire of me and go out . . . for good'), though this is the kind of hope you can arrive at by enumerating possibilities, without evidence that the opposite possibility may not eventuate instead: 'You might get angry and blaze me clean out of my wits. Mightn't you?' It is the culmination of what we have been calling Beckett's Gestapo theme, the spotlight borrowed from Nazi inquisitors and administrators of the American 'third degree'.

We are in no realistic place, however. The three heads before

us belong to bodies immobilized in urns, the heads themselves
are immobile, the voices are toneless, the faces 'so lost to age
and aspect as to seem part of the urns'. All this compels our
attention on the little that will vary, namely the utterance.
There is nothing else on which the distractible mind may linger.

And proceedings are ritualized here. Dim spots on all three
faces elicit a chorus, all three speaking together in low voices,
enlightening neither to the inquisitor nor to us. After
a five-second blackout (it seems an eternity) strong spots on
all three faces provoke the opening phrases of all three narratives, all simultaneous again, all in voices of 'normal strength';
from which the audience may begin to intuit a correlation
between intensity of speech and of light. But as for intelligibility of speech, stronger light alone has not helped, since it has
fallen on all three. There is another blackout, and the spot,
as though collecting its wits, concentrates on the right-hand
head:

W 1: I said to him, give her up. I swore by all I held most sacred—

But the spot does not wait to hear what she swore; it swivels
to the left-hand head:

W 2: One morning. . . .

This promising narrative beginning is interrupted after four
sentences, and the spot swings to the hapless face in the centre:

M: We were not long together. . . .

'Give her up'. 'Give him up'. 'Give up that whore'. These
injunctions appear, one apiece, in the first three speeches,
and we cannot doubt that they converge on a common topic.
Gradually we make out what happened, a banal story of wife,
husband and mistress, and though the theatre audience will
almost certainly never notice it, the reader of the printed text
may easily discover that all three narratives are each of them
continuous. The quickest way for a reader with a book to get
the hang of *Play* is therefore to read straight through
the speeches of each character, one by one. W 1, given to seeing

herself in various dramatic lights ('Judge then of my astoundment when one fine morning, as I was sitting stricken in the morning room . . . '—very elegant banality), was perhaps the wife, or anyway the Wronged Woman. W 2, whose diction is also patent-leather ('Fearing she was about to offer me violence, I rang for Erskine and had her shown out'), was the Other Woman. M, the man, hiccups periodically, which prevents his cutting as fine a rhetorical figure as they. He is silly and vain and riffles with contemptuous satisfaction the clichés of smug penitence ('At home all heart to heart, new leaf and bygones bygones'). He practises a profession—something new in the Beckett cosmos—and W 1 can propose 'a little jaunt to celebrate, to the Riviera or our darling Grand Canary'. Since we know that W 2 keeps a butler, we may judge that affluence insulates all three from the dribbling privations of the Winnies and Willies. The women make silly scenes, however; there are threats of settled hash, of violence; the wife, after her husband's repentance, strolls over to the mistress to 'have a gloat', only to be once more shown out by Erskine. It is all very banal, drawing-room melodrama, cheapened and accelerated. And then something happened.

Unsurprisingly, just what happened is unclear, and anyhow unimportant. M's version (twice repeated) is, 'I simply could no longer—'. W 2's is, 'When he stopped coming . . . '. W 1's is, 'Before I could do anything he had disappeared'. What he could do no longer, amusingly enough, was satisfy them both. His relationships were thoroughly physical, so much so that W 1's first feeling, on learning for sure that while attending to her he was seeing another woman also, was 'of wonderment. What a male!' So we are not to suppose that it was the moral strain that drove him underground. It was the need to recuperate. And neither of them saw him again.

The wife supposed he had run off to the mistress, but after some weeks drove by her rival's place and found it bolted and barred, 'all grey with frozen dew'. 'On the way back by Ash and Snodland', her narrative continues, but what happened on the way back we never learn. A traffic accident? Anyway

here she is. And here he is (by what route?). And here is the
mistress too, who remembers how after she was sure he was
gone out of her life she made a bundle of his things and burned
them, and smelt them smouldering all night.

And here they all are, rehearsing this empty tale for ever.
None of them knows the other two are nearby. Each one supposes the others are alive, up there, elsewhere (and is this
place death?). The rituals of the place continue; a new blackout, a new set of themes, and the shifting of the voices from
the key of Then to the key of Now. They cope with Now
variously, being of various natures. W 1 screams at the light
to get off her, and wonders what she must do to satisfy it. ('Is
it that I do not tell the truth, is that it, that some day somehow I may tell the truth at last and then no more light at last, for
the truth?') But the truth is not in her. She cannot forego,
each time round, the old postures, the old jealous contempt,
or savouring the day she went round to 'have a gloat', or asking
'What he could have found in her when he had me . . . '. She
is an unrelaxing woman, and one understands his recourse
to the other. Her version, she is impregnably sure, is *the* version
('Yes, and the whole thing there, all there, staring you in the
face. You'll see it. Get off me. Or weary.') No, she does
not really tell the truth, though doubtless she tells the facts.

W 2 is sure that the light must know she is doing her best,
and also wonders if she is perhaps a little unhinged (she means
this for a hopeful thought, that she may go mad). She may;
her last two utterances—this should grip the nerves of the
audience—are peals of 'wild low laughter'.

As for M, the poor brute, he supposes that he can dissolve
the past by stating its unimportance. ('I know now, all that
was just . . . play.') He fancies the women drawn together
by their common grief at losing him (him!), just as he remembers
fancying a happy bigamousness, 'the first to wake to wake
the other two'. By 'we were not civilized' he means, the cad,
that the women did not conspire to comply with his desires.
'Such fantasies. Then. And now—'. And now, 'When will
all this have been . . . just play?' For he can suppose that

Hell itself will turn out to be a game, just such a game as he played, without scruple, with hearts.

That is the two-part play, with its light-enforced rite of Then and Now. Whereupon, amazingly, the final chorus turns out to be the opening chorus again, and the players are obeying a stage direction which reads, *Repeat play exactly*. This is possible for the actors, but not for the audience; the second time, the audience is seeing a new work. It understands, the second time, the little hints that before were so many clues to be seized with strained attention, and its understanding is suffused by a new and terrible understanding that these three people are compelled to enact this two-part rite perhaps forever. (And through how many run-throughs will we be kept sitting here?) It is a cunning device. We need the second enactment to understand, fully, the first, and we need it also to grasp the nature of this undeviating hell. How often, in Beckett's work, a two-part structure has suggested an indefinite recurringness: *Godot*, in which 'nothing happens, twice',[16] *Molloy*, in which Moran, at the end of part two, seems about to recommence the career traversed by Molloy in part one, perhaps himself to be sought by yet a new Moran, *Happy Days* in which all is to be done again, Act II differing from Act I chiefly in that Winnie has lost the use of her arms; and Krapp, of course, Krapp playing that ancient tape again, and yet again, and a third time. The players in *Play* are like sentient tape recorders, switched on and off at whim but never changing a word. And it was somehow to be expected that Beckett should eventually devise a two-part structure of exact recurrence, though no audience, as Heraclitus foretold, steps twice into the same stream.

The French text, *Comédie*, contains a curious variant: a footnote gives the producer the option of repeating the play exactly, or else of allowing us to suppose that the repetition is not exact because the light—of all things—is growing tired. This possibility occurred to Beckett during a London production in 1964, and he liked it well enough to repeat it in a Paris production he supervised. The level of the light drops, and its order of solicitation is altered at the director's whim. The voices consequently drop in volume, and while the speeches are rigorously unvaried, they come in altered sequence. It is doubtful if the audience would detect the altered sequence, but it will detect, certainly, the light's fatigue, lending substance to the hope of W 2 that it will one day go out altogether, but lending substance also to the suspicion of W 1 and M that it is paying them no heed at all. M's last words are, 'Am I as much as . . . being seen?'

Yes, of course, of course he is; *we* are seeing him; the light works on *our* behalf. No one's desire to learn what is going on, what has gone on, is more remorseless than ours; strange, when one considers that it is all unreal, all just 'a play'. But of course we always want to know; we are, each of us, on such occasions, monsters of insatiability, and nothing else, in fact, propels a play. How much misery does that rage to find out not also propel! W 1 had to know; she even engaged a detective. As for us, we have bought our tickets. *Hypocrite lecteur*, said Baudelaire, *mon semblable, mon frère*. Beckett says it more obliquely, but says it.

14 Radio, Television, Film

Beckett, the deviser of austere entertainments, has not the entertainer's instinct, which is probably to say, has not the entertainer's ego. Our approval is not the nutriment his gift craves, and there are times when it has accumulated its powers, waiting for a hint. He has been responsive, therefore, to suggestions, as that he should write a play for radio (suggested by the BBC) or a script for a film (suggested by Barney Rosset of the Grove Press). Not all his work by any means has been written at such incentives; the best of it, so far as one knows, has been self-originated. But suggestions—not commissions, since he will not regard an arrangement as binding until he has in fact been able to execute the work—suggestions, then, have led him into adventures with several media he would likely not otherwise have explored. And since the suggestion has specified a medium, not a subject, he has allowed the novel medium to generate its fit subject, achieving thus, with varying success but never without intense interest, a symbiosis between the theme of the work and the kind of experience the audience is having.

Thus in a radio play there is nothing to see, an elementary fact which not all radio dramatists are willing to accept. Much radio drama fights this limitation, looking for ways to offer us mental pictures. Beckett instead made a play about a blind man, and toyed with the odd fact that in a drama exclusively auditory the unheard, unspoken, is the non-existent. *All That Fall*, written in 1956 while he was finishing the French *Endgame*, ends ambiguously according to daytime logic but logically according to the laws of a world where all reality is audible. Dan Rooney has pondered how it would be to murder a child —'nip some young doom in the bud'—and his train came in late because a child, as we learn at the end, slipped down under the wheels, and yet it seems meaningless to ask whether he pushed her there; for the very journey, since it occupies no air-time, is sheer illusion conjured up for us by his telling of what he chooses to tell, a telling according to which he did nothing at all except experience bladder distress. This epistemological point remains faintly irritating however intimate our acquaintance with the play, but it interferes little with the play's enchantment, dependent as the enchantment is on language, notably the vowel-rich language of the blind man's wife, in counterpoint to her husband's frigid rhetoric.

Knowing how dependent we should be on words, Beckett in his first radio script lavished all his resources of eloquence on shaping the speeches; the work may have relieved him amid *Endgame*'s austerities. And since sound passes even as we hear it, in *All That Fall* all passes, dwindles, falls, as transient as breath.

Her sense of transience is Maddy Rooney's tireless theme. 'Poor woman,' run her first words. 'All alone in that ruinous old house.' (And observe the vowels the actress can caress.) The 'poor woman's' existence is attested by a record she is playing, 'Death and the Maiden'. Maddy is herself in decay, 'destroyed', she says, 'with sorrow and pining and gentility and churchgoing and fat and rheumatism and childlessness', reflecting that it is suicide to be abroad and 'a lingering dissolution' to be at home, and though she is 'a great fat jelly', and though one of the high points of the play is the desperate exertion required to get her into a motor car and then to get her out of it, we are oddly aware that all this is a *tour de force* of illusion, that her body does not exist for our senses at all, nor that car, nor anything but objurgations and sounds of effort. All has faded into sound and into incomparable language, and the language itself has the richness of decay.

MRS ROONEY: No no, I am agog, tell me all, then we shall press on and never pause, never pause, till we shall come safe to haven.

Pause.

MR ROONEY: Never pause . . . safe to haven . . . Do you know, Maddy, sometimes one would think you were struggling with a dead language.

MRS ROONEY: Yes indeed, Dan, I know full well what you mean, I often have that feeling, it is unspeakably excruciating.

MR ROONEY: I confess I have it sometimes myself, when I happen to overhear what I am saying.

MRS ROONEY: Well, you know, it will be dead in time, just like our own poor dear Gaelic, there is that to be said.

Her lyric cadenced plaining accompanies us with her the long way to the station, and through the mounting anxiety about the late train and her anxious inability to find her blind husband after the passengers have descended and begun to disappear. Chilling her lyricism, Dan Rooney's first word, spoken on the BBC production in a voice as cold as Stonehenge, is simply 'Maddy'. Another thing he says is, 'We could have saved sixpence. We have saved fivepence. But at what cost?' And another is, 'Once for all, do not ask me to speak and move at the same time. I shall not say this in this life again.' His discourse is as a gelid stream in December, and we know that one more thing that has fallen away in Mrs Rooney's life is reciprocated love. (How often, in a Beckett work, the long-ago death of love has been the crucial event!) In her brief duet with the landscape we sense her terrible isolation:

All is still. No living soul in sight. There is no one to ask. The world is feeding. The wind—(*brief wind*)—scarely stirs the leaves and the birds—(*brief chirp*)—are tired singing. The cows—(*brief moo*)—and sheep—(*brief baa*)—ruminate in silence. The dogs—(*brief bark*)—are hushed and the hens—(*brief cackle*)—sprawl torpid in the dust. We are alone. There is no one to ask.

Silence.

As the rain falls on their homegoing, Dan tells a tale of the train journey, which specifies only that the train stopped mysteriously, and then resumed. ('Say something, Maddy,' he ends, 'Say you believe me.') Beside them a ditch is full of rotting leaves. They erupt into wild laughter at the thought of next Sunday's text, 'The Lord upholdeth all that fall and raiseth up all those that be bowed down.' We learn from a boy—who speaks against Dan Rooney's insistence—about the death of the child. And the last sounds we hear are the sounds of rain, '*Tempest of wind and rain.*'

The parallels with *Endgame* are curious: a tyrannical blind man, the terminal evocation of a doomed child. The ambiguities, in a work where we see nothing though we see Hamm for ninety minutes, are more dissolvent; whether Dan killed that child is unimportant, in fact is an unreal question. Our experience of Dan is what is important, an experience solely of his voice and words, from which we learn that he is a killer at heart, and has killed love, and still keeps his hands clenched about love's throat. Our experience, in this work written, Beckett said, 'to come out of the dark', is of more importance than an implied plot. The mysteries of that plot, residual and troubling, tend if anything to interfere with that experience. In his next radio play, *Embers*, Beckett tried to achieve something less entrancing but more unified, by enclosing the elements of the 'plot' in a deranged man's skull, among numerous other elements.

At this point we should take account of a special frustration. Not only is it difficult to encounter performances of these works for expensive media, it is especially unlikely that we shall encounter adequate performances. A stage play will be more thoroughly rehearsed. It will also be produced a number of times, by different companies, and there is even hope of one director learning from another's mistakes. But radio plays will likely be performed once, and then recorded, a revival therefore re-enacting its flaws as mercilessly as Krapp's time-machine. This is apt to be still more true of a television script, and is eminently true of a film. (There is perhaps no instance in history of a film being produced twice from exactly the same script.) So such productions of these works as have been mounted have acquired an archival quality. In production alone the works live, and yet they are especially vulnerable to production. For instance if the kind of attention they exact is ruptured by any confusion, all is lost, or nearly all.

In the BBC production of 1957, *All That Fall* came across on the whole splendidly. *Embers*, two years later, was less happy, Henry's voice, aged and cracked, being of so stylized a decrepitude that it was difficult in the extreme to make out the words, the all-important words. Since I know of no other performance of *Embers* in English, I can only record that it has been a failure. And yet the script is fascinating.

The reason *Embers* failed entails a problem that has beset Beckett's work since *Endgame*. He has been preoccupied since then with illusion—one pauses to remark that *Happy Days* is the exception—preoccupied with solipsism, with lonely people haunted by interior voices, with peoplings (*How It Is*) that may be the illusions of solitude. And the convention for this illusory plane of reality tends to be something that interferes with intelligibility, in performance if not in the script. Thus it is specified that the voices in *Play* shall be toneless, and the tempo rapid throughout. It is also specified that the sole voice we hear in *Eh Joe* shall be 'low, distinct, remote, little colour'. The voice in *Cascando* is described as 'low, panting', and later as 'weaker'. Since these voices convey virtually all the information we receive, it is evident that the effort of piecing together what we glean from a monologue is greatly compounded by an effort to make out what the words are, and by any subtraction from the script's eloquence of what the actor can do with intonation. Such matters call for a delicacy of producer's judgment that has not always been exercised, and also represent on some occasions downright miscalculation on the author's part. For he has pared each work down to a set of minimal clues, which given the additional impediments to reception are likely to leave the audience more irritated than moved.

Embers depends still more than *All That Fall* on the fact that there is nothing to see. It seems that the protagonist sees only shingle and sea, but spends his time conjuring with sounds and voices in his head, to ward off aloneness. (After *Endgame*, the threat is always aloneness.) 'That sound you hear is the sea,' he tells us. 'I mention it because the sound is so strange, so unlike the sound of the sea, that if you didn't see what it was you wouldn't know what it was.' It is indeed the sea, but we are to learn that he always hears the sea whether he is near it or not, and has the habit of talking, talking, talking, to drown its persistent murmur. He is obsessed by the sea because his father drowned in it. He and Ada made love beside it too. His father's presence now keeps him company, once garrulous but now unspeaking, and Ada keeps him company too, though she speaks. She speaks when he calls her, and seems more bleakly real than his other thoughts, though her movements, unlike his, make no sound. Is she 'there'? We hear her voice, but only after Henry has called on it, and other things we hear —horses' hooves, for instance—come and go as Henry bids. He calls up and banishes sounds, that is a constant in his mental life, and her voice would seem to be something he has called up. So she is unreal, but more real than his now-silent father, or his horses' hooves, and paradoxically less real than the story he tells himself.

When hers was a live voice he loathed it—'Ada too, conversation with her, that was something, that's what hell will be like, small chat to the babbling of Lethe about the good old days when we wished we were dead. (*Pause*.) Price of margarine fifty years ago. (*Pause*.) And now.' He loathed Ada then, he loathed their child, he hated his father who also hated him ('A washout, that's all you are, a washout!' were the last words he heard his father speak in life). His father had long bouts of silent depression, and was last seen sitting unmoving on a rock as if one with the stillness of the great sea he died in. There had been a family upheaval. It was suicide, surely.

These facts come filtering through Henry's solipsism, all pale beside the story he tells himself, a story into which his frozen feelings flow. It is about Bolton, 'an old man in great trouble', and his great trouble goes unspecified. He is waiting before his fire on a winter night ('snow everywhere, bitter cold,

white world') and the man he has sent for comes: Dr Holloway.
The narrative runs on, urgent in its sensate immediacy:

Outside all still, not a sound, dog's chain maybe or a bough groaning
if you stood there listening long enough, white world, Holloway with
his little black bag, not a sound, bitter cold, full moon small and white,
crooked trail of Holloway's galoshes. Vega in the Lyre very green.
(*Pause.*) Vega in the Lyre very green.

'Old men, great trouble, white world, not a sound': this sums
up the first phase of the story. Henry breaks off to express
his own plight, in a world full of ineluctable sounds:

Stories, stories, years and years of stories, till the need came on me,
for someone, to be with me, anyone, a stranger, to talk to, imagine
he hears me, years of that, and then, now, for someone who . . . knew
me, in the old days, anyone, to be with me, imagine he hears me, what
I am, now.

He resumes, projecting his story out of this need. Bolton ('grand
old figure') had called Holloway ('fine old chap') 'in the cold
and dark, an old friend, urgent need, bring the bag'. And
now Bolton will only look into Holloway's eyes, saying 'Please!
PLEASE!'

Henry has his bleak chat with Ada. Her voice (imagined)
tells him (low, remote) what he no doubt has thought of and
thought of, the last hour of his father, how she saw his father
sitting still by the sea on that rock. She tells him (in his head)
why his father (in his head) doesn't answer him any more:

I suppose you have worn him out. (*Pause.*) You wore him out living
and now you are wearing him out dead. (*Pause.*) The time comes
when one cannot speak to you any more. (*Pause.*) The time will come
when no one will speak to you at all, not even complete strangers.
(*Pause.*) You will be quite alone with your voice, there will be no
other voice in the world but yours. (*Pause.*) Do you hear me?

Henry remembers what he had been accustomed to blank out,
the story of how Ada went back to look for his father and saw
no one, and after a while gave up and took the tram home
(his father was drowning then, or newly drowned). The whole

bleak story is of missed opportunities, of absences and avoid-
ances and non-communications, and he reverts to his story of
Bolton and Holloway, that richer reality, under his control.
And the richer reality brings the bleak reality to apotheosis:
Bolton begging for what Holloway cannot give, what no one
can give him since he cannot receive it, communion. He says
'Please!' and 'Please!' and 'Please, Holloway!' but will not,
cannot say what it is he pleads for. Carrying over a candle
he looks Holloway full in the face. He 'won't ask again, just
the look', and Holloway recoiling from that look covers his
face. 'Not a sound, white world, bitter cold, ghastly scene, old
men, great trouble, no good.'

This is Henry talking, the 'washout', the sterile hating man
who vexes the voices of the absent: Henry unfrozen by compassion for his own fiction, which (in a circle fatally closed) is
about an impasse produced by the need for compassion.

Embers, once we have teased it out in this way, may be taken
as the paradigm, for once explicit, of everything Beckett has
done since the late 1950s. It is unusual in presenting so explicitly, albeit enigmatically, the elements of the past situation,
the past happenings, from which the present agony is a recoiling,
of which it is a product, and around which it obsessively re-
volves. The man in *How It Is* had some such past story, re-
fracted through his memories of Pam Prim dying, and the
fantasy, if it is a fantasy, of his dreadful coupling with Pim is
like Henry's story of Bolton and Holloway, a fictive projection
of his urgent need for communion. Compared with *How It Is*,
Embers is curiously old-fashioned, like 'My Last Duchess': a
story that might have been told at great length chronologically,
but folded up into a monologue from which we are to piece its
elements together. How much a radio audience might in fact
piece together remains undetermined. It would assuredly be
worth a new production. But Henry's words would need to
be clearly audible.

One way of clarifying that kind of story would be to let the
voice hammer it at the haunted man straightforwardly, and
dispense with the contrapuntal fantasy. That is the strategy

attempted in *Eh Joe*, twenty minutes for television (1966), a thinner harder work, a remorseless work which imprisons Joe's unspeaking head in a box (the box in our living room) for the eternity in which a woman's voice assails him and the camera moves nearer, nearer. Voices have assailed him before, and he has vanquished them all: his father's, for instance, and his mother's. But this woman persists, and rubs his face one more time in the story he has been at such pains to shut out, having in fact inspected the entire room to be certain he is alone (alone!). It is the story of the suicide of another of the women he seduced and discarded, dying by the strand, a place for her face scooped out in the stones. The special poignance is that she seems to have died not out of rage but out of loneliness, not turned away from his memory but toward it, 'Lips on a stone . . . Taking Joe with her . . . Light gone . . . "Joe Joe" . . . No sound . . . To the stones [. . .] And the hands . . . Before they go . . . Imagine the hands . . . What are they at? . . . In the stones . . .'

Film, twenty-four minutes, substitutes for the ineluctable voice an ineluctable eye. One difference is this, that by turning away from it you can shut out an eye's prying. It is established, moreover, that this is a soundless world, uninvaded by acoustic space. This is established by the film's wittiest touch, the 'sssh!' which is the sole sound on the soundtrack, and posits that we are not in the silent world of the silent films which resulted from the mere unavailability of sound, but in a silent world where sound exists and one nonetheless hears nothing, not a foot-fall.

The protagonist, one of Beckett's haunted clowns like Krapp, 'storms along in comic foundered precipitancy', wearing a long dark overcoat in midsummer and screening his face from our scrutiny. From the camera's scrutiny? Yes, but the camera, moving, probing, in bringing us what we see stands for ourselves. No one can bear that scrutiny. It is as absolute as the spot-light in *Play*, though unlike the spotlight, which compels speech, the eye of the camera, when anyone stares into it, creates an 'agony of perceivedness' that is gauged by the swooning of an old woman after a few seconds' exposure to it. Since it does not trouble animals, we should think of it as an exclusively human agony, perhaps related to conscience.

'Climate of film', says a script note, 'comic and unreal'. The man 'should excite laughter throughout by his way of moving'. So he covers mirror and window in the little room he's been running to, ejects the cat and the dog—a long hilarious sequence, since the one tends to return through the door he opens to put out the other—destroys the Divine Eye on the wall, covers up the great staring eye of the caged parrot and the great magnified eye of the englobed fish; then at last, in an eyeless room, sits down in a chair like Murphy's to rock and to destroy his past.

His past is represented by seven images, of which one at least, the child kneeling in prayer at the knee of his extravagantly hatted mother, was among the repertory of images that visited the man crawling in the mud in *How It Is*. This man's panic-ridden world is like that mud, but unlike the being whose images were mental, this man can handle photographs and tear them to pieces. He turns them through in chronological order—a time-lapse film within a film—allowing us as we look over his shoulder to see him grow from infancy to dour maturity. Then in reverse order, he destroys them, and, disencumbered at last, falls asleep.

Then the camera circles stealthily to obtain the full-face view it had been denied: the ravaged face with the eye-patch. And he awakes and sees it: a ravaged face like his own, *intent*. His features, as he sits frozen in his chair, enact the 'agony of perceivedness' which is self-perception, as when, at the end of *How It Is*, the protagonist's terminal agony is that of being alone. This is the agony Henry in *Embers* evades, the last agony with which the voice threatens Joe. And we are entitled to draw a final conclusion, that if the camera stands for ourselves, and resembles him, then he too is ourselves, evading that gaze. We too, in entering the darkened place where we watch films, all of us facing in the same direction, have sought refuge from all eyes including our own; and we too, when the perceiving face looks intently out toward us from the screen, encounter in amazement ourselves.

In the film as it was produced in 1964 all this is shaky. Beckett's script professes frank uncertainty about cinematic devices, Alan Schneider had never directed a film before nor Grove Press produced one, there was too little time available in the inter-locking schedules of indispensable people, and Buster Keaton, a hero of the author's from the 1920s, proved to be irritated by the esoteric conception until, late in the shooting, about the time of the ejection of the animals, it began to catch his fancy. Mainly, the crucial distinction between the two kinds of images—the protagonist's perception of the room, the camera's perception of him perceiving—was insufficiently em-phatic to be recognized at once as a convention. The de-focused images that stand for his perception seem at first like slight mistakes. More attention to a convention of highlights rayed like stars (and more money, more time) might have helped. A philosophical film which is in part about the order of escape we are indulging in when we go film-watching remains a con-ception of potential interest, and one wishes that, like a play whose first production has been unsatisfactory, it could be realized anew. But there was only one Keaton.

Words and Music (1962) and *Cascando* (1963) differ radically from all these other works in having no realistic content what-ever. Abandoning the order of 'plot' which makes *Embers* so difficult, they open themselves to the unspecifying quality of broadcast sound, to the documentary uses of which they are related as to a newspaper report a Symbolist poem. *Words and Music* in particular resembles an intricate rich Symbolist poem composed in a medium still more suggestive than Mal-larmé's printed language, a medium of pure audition. It is the most profound, the most original use to which Beckett has put radio, and one is tempted to say as original and moving a use as any to which radio has been put. I regret that I have only an intuitive base for this judgment. I have no idea how the music is meant to sound—John Beckett's score for *Words and Music* is unpublished and Marcel Mihalovici's for *Cascando* inaccessible to me—and I have never heard a performance of either work.

We are not to expect analytical 'meaning' of a drama one of whose protagonists is a small orchestra (*Music*) and the other a voice of great flexibility, called *Words*. There is a third voice, named *Croak*, for whom they are as persons, named respectively Joe and Bob. They are his 'comforts', and he bids them 'be friends', but their tendency is to be exasperated by one another. *Words* has been rehearsing a turgid discourse on sloth, but *Croak*, obsessed by a face, on the stairs, in the tower (what a Gothic decor! only workable because mental), announces that tonight's theme shall be love, so *Words* hastily adapts his oration.

Love is of all the passions the most powerful passion and indeed no passion is more powerful than the passion of love. (*Clears throat.*) This is the mode in which the mind is most strongly affected and indeed in no mode is the mind more strongly affected than in this. . . .

When last we heard him gabble this scholastic garbage the operative noun was not love but sloth, which suggests that in his mind, or *Croak's* (since in the acoustic space of radio-drama they may be thought of as sharing a mind), these passions seem allied in dangerousness. *Croak* demands a musical treatment instead. He is treated to 'soft music worthy of foregoing', whatever 'worthy of foregoing' may mean. It grows clear that *Words'* specifyings are unwelcome to *Croak* on this subject, that *Music's* expressiveness is balm; music has the power of conveying passion without the awkward questionings about danger to the soul.

That is all about love. *Croak* announces a new theme, age. *Words* has no set speech ready, but gradually, in reluctant collaboration with *Music*, he evolves an ashen song; age is when

> She comes in the ashes
> Who loved could not be won
> Or won not loved
> Or some other trouble
> Like in that old light

> The face in the ashes
> That old starlight
> On the earth again.

And that is all about age. Then *Croak* announces the third theme, 'The face', the face, we surmise, that he saw on the stairs in the tower. *Words* embarks on a frigid description; we may remember the eyes narrowed to slits that gazed up at Krapp, or the pale eyes—'spirit made light'—of the dying girl that haunts the man in *Eh Joe*. It is a face that has been haunting *Croak* 'at all hours', often, in recent months, in cloud and shine; he has examined it, we sense, remotely, as though immersed in sloth. 'Leaving aside the features of lineaments proper, matchless severally and in their ordonnance': such phrasing conveys the detachment of his inspection. Krapp had striven in the same way to remain detached. But this corpse-like face, corresponding we gather to the deadness of his cold preoccupation, can come to life; meaning that love long dormant in him can come to life? Yet the resurrection, like the Gothic decor, has a touch of Poe:

the brows uncloud, the lips part and the eyes ... (*pause*) ... the brows uncloud, the nostrils dilate, the lips part and the eyes ... (*pause*) ... a little colour comes back into the cheeks and the eyes ... (*reverently*) ... open. (*Pause.*) Then down a little way.... (*Pause....*)

Croak has cried 'No!' at the prospect of her awakening. He stays silent to hear the song they compose in its honour, *Music* leading with discreet suggestions; it culminates:

> Down a little way
> To whence one glimpse
> Of that wellhead.

The effect on *Croak* is cataclysmic. To shocked cries of 'My Lord!' he shuffles off, unable to bear the explicitness, the awakening, the evocation of the 'wellhead'. He shuffles off, one gathers, to the solitude where he cherishes his psychic necrophilia, where love and sloth are one. *Words*, moved by their joint eloquence, is left to beg *Music* to play it again. Their dissonances are composed, and *Words*, chill *Words*, is overwhelmed. The last sound we hear is his sigh.

There is powerful insight here, the aesthetic faculties conspiring to deliver a vision their possessor cannot face. In *Cascando* (which means diminishing volume, decreasing tempo, and is also the title of one of Beckett's two or three best poems, written in 1935) a man who is very confident of his command of both the verbal and the musical faculties opens them, closes them, singly and together, aware that he is incomprehensible to censorious folk called 'they'.

They say, That is not his life, he does not live on that. They don't see me, they don't see what my life is, they don't see what I live on, and they say, That is not his life, he does not live on that.
Pause.
I have lived on it . . . till I'm old.
Old enough.
Listen.

His life is the familiar one, the telling of stories in a voice that hopes, at last, to be achieving the last story. The difference in *Cascando*, is that music is at his disposal as well, and the script unfortunately, unlike that of *Words and Music*, gives no indication whatever of the music's character. (There is specified music, Mihalovici's, with which by contract the play must be performed; it is to be borrowed from Huegel et Cie. Paris.) The story is about Woburn (called Maunu in the French original), fleeing, stumbling, sprawling in mud, then sprawling face down in a boat drifting by night, oarless, tillerless, his back to the stars, out to the open sea. The story is not the theme; the theme is the contrast between the self-enwrapped detachment of the presiding mind, his awareness of what 'they' say, his studied indifference to 'them', between this and the impassioned anxiety of his narrative voice to catch up with Woburn,

—sleep . . . no more stories . . . come on . . . Woburn . . . it's him . . . see him . . . say him . . . to the end. . . don't let go . . . .

'I've got him . . . nearly' this voice encourages itself; it follows Woburn, apparently, into extinction; its last words are 'come on ... come on'. It ceases, and simultaneously the music ceases too. The last direction is '*Silence*'. The presiding mind, it is clear, does not 'tell' his story, he permits it to emerge, an eruption, unbidden from his inner dark. His metaphor is of opening and of closing, not of telling: simply switching the story and its music on and off. The story is his life, and something not himself also.

15   Come and Go

'A Dramaticule', says the title-page of this last stage work
to date, written in 1965. Vi, Flo and Ru, three characters
again; but unlike the three people in *Play*, who were at each
other's throats, the three women in *Come and Go* (with an
unstated epigraph by Eliot: In the room the women come
and go/Talking of Michelangelo), are delicately solicitous of
one another's susceptibilities, and do not chatter of Michelangelo at all but define themselves by what they do not say.
Each is (we gather) doomed. (We all are, but less proximately.)
Each engages in conversation with her neighbour about the
symptoms of the third. Each is very emphatic that nothing
untoward shall be said: no cattiness, no gloating. They have
a past in common—the playground at Miss Wade's, when
they were three little maids from school; a present aspect in
common, which is like that of the weird sisters in *Macbeth*
and is hinted at in the first line, 'When did we three last meet?',
recalling the other play's opening: When shall we three meet
again, In thunder, lightning or in rain?—and a present decorum
in common, which is summarized in the second spoken sentence:
'Let us not speak.'

And they share a fantasy, that, holding hands, they feel
rings on one another's fingers, though the text explicitly states
that no rings are visible. It is a beautiful, delicate, decorous
work; if the scale of the action falls below the 'certain magnitude' Aristotle specified, well, so much the worse; and if there
is no way to make it the culmination of a theatrical evening,
it is a pity we demand so much of a theatre evening. It would

be a nice exercise, to devise a programme to which *Come and Go* might serve as finale, neither overwhelmed nor coarsened by the rest of the bill. It is a play made of what they do not say: of silence, of silences. I have written almost three times as many words as the text contains.

16 Queer Little Pieces

Suddenly, in the mid-1960s, ultra-compression became Beckett's norm. *Come and Go* (1966), as this is written his last play with lines for people to speak, occupies three minutes (121 words, 23 speeches, 12 silences). The rigorous attention to detail included watercolour on bits of paper pinned to the typescript to prescribe the muted colours of the costumes. The less there is, the more everything matters. Subsequently he offered *Breath*, not a play but a happening, a hardly-happening. And labours of which jettisoned manuscripts in research collections[17] afford only a sampling have eventuated from time to time in strange little prose pieces, say three to five pages. They exact a new order of attention, entailing as they do the reconstruction of whole worlds out of minimal fragments. We examine one as a geologist might the sole piece of some exploded planet, a pertinent analogy since *Imagination Dead Imagine* for one, and *Ping* and *The Lost Ones* for two others, are residua of two vaster works (novels? what is a novel?).

Thus *Enough* (1965) begins, 'All that goes before forget', as though to explain why all that goes before is missing, and proceeds to recall 'my' relationship with 'him', and what became of it. The relationship was a compounding of grotesqueries, congruent enough to specify, perhaps, the customs of an alien planet. Or no, it is earth, the terrestrial equator is mentioned, though there were also 'times I discerned on the horizon a sea whose level seemed higher than ours', which sounds not earthly. The weather was 'eternally mild. As if the earth had come to rest in spring.' There was no more wind, though 'he' could remember wind. Sudden rains fell 'without noticeable darkening of the sky'. Flowers seem to have been everywhere, 'stemless and flat on the ground like water-lilies'. There is no mention of other people. This went on for years.

'He' took me by the hand when 'I' was six years old, and was 'very bowed' then. As grotesque a fact as the world in question affords is his later configuration: his trunk parallel to the ground, his legs spraddled and bent, his feet 'flat and splay'. His horizon, therefore, was 'the ground they trod', and he inspected the stars, when he did so, with the aid of a mirror. 'One day he halted and fumbling for his words explained to me that anatomy is a whole.'

To reconstruct his experience, therefore, entails geometrical visualizations. We are to imagine how he climbed steep hills ('On a gradient of one in one his head swept the ground'), and from this information and from a single sentence—'The crest once reached alas the going down again'—we must envisage the anomalies of equilibrium signalled by 'alas'. 'All I know comes from him', and his discourse was largely mathematical:

What mental calculations bent double hand in hand! Whole ternary numbers raised in this way to the third power sometimes in downpours of rain. Graving themselves in his memory as best they could ensuing cubes accumulated. In view of the converse operation at a latter stage. When time would have done its work.

If the work of time would be to erase memories, then from the graven cubes the forgotten cube roots could again have been—to yield what satisfaction?—extracted.

Two events stand out: the day he conjectured that his deformity had 'reached its peak', the day, some ten years later (say 7,000 miles of walking), when he told me to leave and I did: still unsure if I understood this injunction correctly.

The narrator is still obsessed by him, by him only. The narrator's sex is indeterminate. The final sentence alludes to 'my old breasts' which in fantasy 'feel his old hand', though an earlier sentence has had us, when recumbent, turning over 'as one man': perhaps simply an idiom, but anyway something to visualize. The whole is grotesque, fragile, pathetic, the tone novel in its broken resigned persistence. And it is Beckett's last work in the first person, which he had employed in fiction for twenty years.

Or not quite his last. *Imagination Dead Imagine* (also 1965) has a narrator, though the stress is on what he sees. This text is the residuum of a novel, one Poe might have conceived, or a fantasist of space travel. Clearly we are on another world, where in the midst of whiteness a white rotunda, measurements specified, contains two bodies, a man and a woman, unanimated, curled into the tight space, on their right sides 'back to back head to arse'. The explorer-narrator renders his observations with precision, supplying letters to help us diagram the semi-circles in which these beings are 'inscribed'. 'Hold a mirror to their lips, it mists'; and the eyes open at incalculable intervals 'and gaze in unblinking exposure long beyond what is humanly possible.' 'The bodies seem whole and in fairly good condition to judge by the surfaces exposed to view.' Light and temperature drop at intervals to blackness and freezing, then return to glare and fierce heat. This takes some twenty seconds either way, and contrary to normal physical laws the temperature does not lag behind the light. The source of the fierce light is unascertainable; it floods the place so that the white rotunda vanishes into the white plain.

Leave them there, sweating and icy, there is better elsewhere. No, life ends and no, there is nothing elsewhere, and no question now of ever finding again that white speck lost in whiteness, to see if they still lie still in the stress of that storm, or of a worse storm, or in the black dark for good, or the great whiteness unchanging, and if not what they are doing.

This sentence, the last, may mean that the white-on-white is irrecoverable once you have wandered away from it, but it seems meant to be connected with the first sentence:

No trace anywhere of life, you say, pah, no difficulty there, imagination not dead yet, yes, dead, good, imagination dead imagine.

And we may choose to connect the whole with a passage in *How It Is*, where we read:

the voice quaqua on all sides then within in the little vault empty closed eight planes bone-white if there were a light a tiny flame all would be white ten words fifteen words like a fume of sighs when the panting stops then the storm the breath token of life part three and last it must be nearly ended

Either white enclosure is like a skull's interior. Are they then, those still ones, the dormant imagination? Is the project to describe the conditions that make a subject inconceivable?

After this, in the work of which *Ping* and *The Lost Ones* are our tokens, we get the third person exclusively, in a strange bleak externality of denotation. *Ping* has not even verbs, simply specifications. It exists, some being exists, in a condition of enclosure, strange light, strange heat, floor and ceiling each a yard square and united by walls each two yards high: a minimal cell for a man. The interior of this space is white (though no one to describe it could get in there with him), the body likewise white, 'white on white invisible', but eyes light blue. He hangs like a puppet, fixed; from time to time the word 'ping', like a bell, precedes (effects?) a transition from 'fixed' to 'fixed elsewhere', whatever that may mean. We also find 'ping murmur ping silence'. Phrases recur hypnotically, the same yet not always quite the same, so that reading the text is like scanning frame after frame of film for the infinitesimal differences that signify change. There is minimal change, sudden and stimulated by 'ping'. A photograph exists of Samuel Beckett scanning strips of film in New York, 1964, during the filming of *Film*, and the novel of which *Ping* is a residuum was begun late the next year. This prompts a guess about *Ping's* origins, maybe a helpful guess. It is pertinent to the emphasis on lighting, the absence of details as though in overexposure, and does help explain what has become of the verbs. Each frame of a film is *so*, like a noun, and the action, normally specified by verbs, is an illusion generated by the frames' successiveness.

In *The Lost Ones*, said to be a fragment of the same abandoned project, we are restricted to the anatomy of an environment: a cylindrical interior, mysteriously lighted and pervaded by breathing sounds and by rapid oscillations of temperature. It is inhabited by 'bodies', one per square yard or say two hundred all told, who (1) circulate unceasingly, or (2) circulate with brief halts, or (3) stay still until disturbed, or (4) never move. These four categories are exhaustive. There are ladders leading to niches, which some climb despite the random gaps in the rungs. The fifteen unnumbered divisions of the text concentrate on various aspects of this environment and the customs of its inhabitants, with constant unemphatic repetition of details from other sections, again in the manner of film shots which establish themselves with respect to one another by bits of overlapping information.

This relentless externality, in which no one speaks and the very words before us seem not to be spoken, not really even written except as computer printouts may be said to have been written, show us Beckett worlds in a new way, with emphasis on the highly special physical arrangements. He has always imagined odd environments congruent with the goings-on: the room in *Endgame* with its trash-cans, the jars in *Play* with their spotlights, Mr. Knott's unvisualizable house, the city in *Molloy* with its ramparts and narrow entrances through enormous vaults, the room in which Malone dies, which appears (to Malone) to vary in dimension, and to move about within a building of varying scale. Always these environments were accessory to the human action. In *Ping* and *The Lost Ones* we are to imagine the opposite, and in *Imagination Dead Imagine* also: a setting so overwhelming, so arbitrary, so referrable to mechanical superintendence perhaps, or to unknown physical laws, that it determines what little can occur. Are these cells of some nether hell? And yet they are always enclosed, like a brain. And neither long work got beyond some condensed pages, as though Beckett had tried (as usual) to do what proved this time impossible, protract a narrative in the absence of happenings.

Lessness (published in French as *Sans*, 1969) cycles and recycles allotropic sentences of about a dozen words each through a gravely moving ritual. The first paragraph runs,

Ruins true refuge long last towards which so many false time out of mind. All sides endlessness earth sky as one no stir not a breath. Grey face two pale blue little body heart beating only upright. Blacked out fallen open four walls over backwards true refuge issueless.

Ruins for refuge, and a bleak outer world: this is no such contrived and functioning hell as *Ping* and *The Lost Ones* depicted, but the aftermath of a cataclysm. It continues its orderly chant of ruins and featurelessness, the statements grouped in paragraphs, twenty-four of them. In the insistence of recurrent elements the most casual reader will sense that there is no sentence that does not contain elements common to many others; the persistent reader may discover moreover that every sentence occurs verbatim twice, once in the first half of the work, once in the second. We are in the midst of an orderly permutation like the lists in *Watt*, but a permutation whose effect is not that of compulsiveness, rather like that of the permuted words in a sestina. Compare two successive stanzas of a sestina from Sidney's *Arcadia*:

STREPHON: Me seemes I see the high and stately mountaines,
  Transforme themselves to lowe dejected vallies:
  Me seemes I heare in these ill-changed forrests,
  The nightingales doo learne of Owles their musique:
  Me seemes I feele the comfort of the morning
  Turnde to the mortal serene of an evening.

KLAIUS: Me seemes I see a filthie cloudie evening,
  As soone as Sunne begins to climbe the mountaines:
  Me seemes I feel a noisome scent, the morning
  When I do smell the flowers of these vallies:
  Me seemes I heare, when I doo heare sweet musique,
  The dreadful cries of murdered men in forrests. . . .

Six words, repeated, systematically permuted, 'circumscribe', wrote William Empson,[18] the world of Klaius and Strephon; and 'in tracing their lovelorn pastoral tedium through thirteen repetitions, with something of the aimless multitudinousness of the sea on a rock, we seem to extract all the meaning possible from these notions.' The tedium of *Lessness* is neither lovelorn nor pastoral; *Lessness* is like a sestina for the atomic age, its unit not the word but the whole sentence, whole sentences interchanging molecular phrases, and the order of the whole in part rationalizable, in part ascribable to a random number generator. The disaster it laments is massive and public. Ten of its sentences, marked by the phrase 'true refuge', affirm the collapse of that refuge. Ten, marked by the words 'earth' and 'sky', affirm an outer featurelessness. Ten employ the phrase 'little body', ten more the phrase 'all gone from mind', ten, denying past and future, employ the word 'never' (except one which uses instead the phrase 'figment dawn'). Ten, finally, venture to make an affirmation, and their sign is the future tense.[19] And, borrowing other phrases from one another, these sixty sentences are so arranged that the emotional density is fairly uniform throughout. The whole goes nowhere but round and through itself, like the molecules in a gas. And what is there more coherent, it seems to say, about a certain order of thinkable public reality? It probably has not a single speaker, more likely the collective voice of a tribe. Searching their utterance for signs of hope, we find among the future-tense statements, 'It will be day and night again over him the endlessness the air heart will beat again'; and also, sardonically, the last of these hopeful utterances, near the end of the penultimate paragraph: 'He will curse God again as in the blessed days face to the open sky the passing deluge.'

17 Retrospect

What is there at last to be said about all this? For one thing
—surprisingly—that it is an old-fashioned coherent *oeuvre*,
the kind of Collected Works that will some day be edited with
'variants' and the display of parallel texts in two languages.
Beckett's sensibility is profoundly conservative, and nowhere
is he more traditional than in his regard for the integrity of
the printed work, the scrupulousness of its phrasing, the accuracy
of its proof-reading, the exemplary adequacy of the translations.
How It Is being punctuated by the voids between paragraphs,
he laboured at his page-proofs to ensure that when such a void
coincided with a page-ending and flowed into the white space
at the bottom of the leaf, the line of type just above it should
never be full, since that would produce an unwanted ambiguity
as to whether a spell of utterance had ended or not. On such
minutiae, and on each sentence, he brings to bear a single-
minded intensity not different in quality from the attention he
devotes to a twenty-minute play or indeed a full-length novel.

When it is not the void, his unit of effect is the sentence,
articulated with the care of a Symbolist poem. This care for
the sentence is itself very nearly revolutionary. The English
writer's unit of effect, when it has been something briefer than
the episode, for nearly two centuries has been the phrase.
Dickens, Tennyson, Bernard Shaw, T. S. Eliot—four writers
alike only in being celebrated in their times—were all phrase-
makers. Their sentences, though orthodox to be sure, served
chiefly to legitimize the phrase. Tennyson's phrase, 'immemorial

elms' is remembered. Who remembers the sentence in which
it is embedded?

A phrase, the interaction of a few words, is an achievement
like a chemist's, something glowing unexpectedly in a vial.
A sentence is an achievement of a different order: a construction
like a Roman arch or the great circle in a geodesic dome, a
directed interdependency, carrying the attention between points
of reference which are themselves the termini of other sentences.
Malone writes of the being he is creating in his notebook,

> It is right that he too should have his little chronicle, his memories,
> his reason, and be able to recognize the good in the bad, the bad in
> the worst, and so grow gently old down all the unchanging days, and
> die one day like any other day, only shorter.

—a flawless rhythmic structure pregnant with grotesqueries.

By applying the proverbial injunction to discern 'good' amid
'bad', the phrasemaker's wit has made 'bad' shine amid 'worst'.
Such wit would have sufficed most authors, but Beckett is not
content until his *trouvaille* has been located within a formal
arc, which as its cadence is nearing resolution two surprising
words terminate and undercut: 'only shorter'! The deadly
effect of these two words needs that ample syntactic scale.
They play against 'one day like any other day' as 'the bad in
the worst' plays against 'the good in the bad', and 'grow gently
old' against 'unchanging days': traditional phrases, familiar
quotations, accorded the courtesy of more than routine attention though the upshot of that courtesy is to leave them less
potent than they had seemed. Like Archimedes, Beckett needs
a long lever and a standpoint. His standpoint is his intent
syntactic orthodoxy. 'Ah, the old questions,' cries Hamm,
'the old answers, there's nothing like them.' There's nothing
like them indeed, and much of Beckett's intellectual vigour
is devoted to defining curious voids between their shape and
their applicability. He has said that he will sit motionless two
or three hours at his writing-table, trying to 'descend into the
darkness'. Once down in the dark, though, where traditions
are queried, he is taut with vigilance.

To query the traditional is still to use it, and one tradition Beckett uses even as he undercuts it is the old premise of the Symbolist poets, the admission of no random words, no unimportant sentences. This entails also writing no unnecessary piece, nothing that repeats what you have done before, nothing redundant. Again his rigour proves subversive. Though such a programme implies plenary competence, he has managed to infect each new construction with doubt: doubt of his ability to accomplish it, doubt of its value if it can be accomplished. Can *Endgame* possibly be protracted? Possibly be ended? —so we may ask in the theatre, moment by moment. And what was it anyway? we may wonder as we leave. So the utmost in local finish—those flawless sentences again—comports with a radical uncertainty, as though to signal the termination of the old Renaissance artist's role, monarch (like Hamm) of his local creation.

Joyce, of whom he never speaks without reverence, is Beckett's personifier of that role. 'The more Joyce knew,' Beckett has remarked, 'the more he could.' And Joyce said that every syllable in his work could be justified. 'That is one way to write,' remarks Beckett, 'but not the only way.' Joyce is also on record as having discovered that he could do anything he wished with language. This can be put another way: he wished to do just what he could. His aspirations and his capacities were coterminous, and patience, application, attention, would suffice to complete to his satisfaction any project he might embark on. Thus the neoclassic critical schema—what did the artist set out to do, how well did he do it?—exactly fits Joyce's procedures, and if his grade is ever less than alpha plus, that is because, being human, he sometimes nodded, the way Horace said Homer nodded. One of his problems was that he couldn't always read his own notes, an executant's difficulty not at all inherent in his enterprise.

For such an art—to simplify its assumptions—is an art of execution. Joyce noted of a tenor he admired that in a certain opera he surmounted 456 G's, 93 A-flats, 54 B-flats, 15 B's, 19 C's, and 2 C-sharps. 'No one else can do it.' No one else, either, could have written a page of *Finnegans Wake*, the challenges of which might have been schematized likewise. Shakespeare's assumptions may not have been very different. If he desired this man's art and that man's scope, still it was thinkable that one might command those endowments, and then be able to undertake what they permitted. And novels especially have seemed separable into orders of accomplishment, that of inventing the story and its tone, that of filling the pages. It is easy to assume that to make art is to accomplish what you have first conceived. About 1949, in a series of prose Dialogues with Georges Duthuit, Samuel Beckett challenged this very assumption.

The ostensible subject of these Dialogues is painting, a manageable metaphor for any art. The speaker called 'B' (Beckett) states that the great Renaissance painters 'surveyed the world with the eyes of building contractors', and 'never stirred from the field of the possible, however much they may have enlarged it.' And a twentieth-century 'revolutionary' painter, a Matisse for instance, does not differ in this respect from Leonardo. He disturbs nothing but 'a certain order on the plane of the feasible'.

Can there be any other plane for the maker? asks 'D' (Duthuit).

'Logically none,' replies 'B'. 'Yet I speak of an art turning from it in disgust, weary of its puny exploits, weary of pretending to be able, of being able, of doing a little better the same old thing, of going a little further along a dreary road.'

What will such an art prefer?

'The expression that there is nothing to express, nothing with which to express, nothing from which to express, no power to express, no desire to express, together with the obligation to express.'

This formula, incapacity combined with obligation, gives us The Unnamable's plight, what we have called the Gestapo convention. It is also the plight of Lucky ('Think, pig!') and of Krapp, whose birthday ritual calls for a new recording to express his present state, the recording he savagely terminates, ripping the tape from the machine, in order to hear and rehear the accents that emanate from a lost Paradise, though when he recorded it thirty years ago it did not seem a Paradise but a document.

An Oriental art then, stripped, its inner subject emptiness?

No. To long for a diminished art, an austerity of spaces and intervals, is still to undergo two familiar maladies, 'the malady of wanting to know what to do and the malady of wanting to be able to do it'. The void, even, can turn into an assignment.

We may discern a principle here, since no assignment can be perfectly completed. Art always fails, even *Hamlet* is not what it might be, but we do not speak of that. We speak of approximations to success, and rank the author of *Hamlet* in a high percentile. But if we reflect on Beckett's assertions in the Dialogues, still more if we reflect on Beckett's works, we may discern a principle which will not disregard the inevitable component of failure, but will embrace it.

Here an analogy may help. It follows from a logic most of us have inherited that Nature too always fails, though we seldom say so. For whenever we attempt an experiment we may see Nature striving to live up to the tidy laws of the physicist, and never succeeding. Galileo tells us how weights fall in a vacuum, accelerating at 32 feet per second per second regardless of their mass. But if we try it, clumsy Nature will deliver at best an approximation to this norm. We shall be told that we must correct for air resistance, for spin, for presented surface, for numerous factors Nature seems unable to avoid dragging in. When Newton tells us that a moving body persists in its movement unless interfered with, we deduce that a wheel once set spinning will spin for ever. But no, it turns out that we must correct for countless drags, including the impingement of the very light by which the wheel is discerned (how resourceful Nature seems to be with excuses!). Physics in general posits a world in which we can have no experiences, and then tells us what the experiences would be like could we have them. And similarly Art posits unachievable feats, which we learn to appraise as though they had been achieved, thus accrediting facile triumphs.

By contrast, Beckett in the third Dialogue proposes a new situation for the artist, and a new act:

The situation is that of him who is helpless, cannot act, in the end cannot paint, since he is obliged to paint. The act is of him who, helpless, unable to act, acts, in the event paints, since he is obliged to paint.
D.—Why is he obliged to paint?
B.—I don't know.
D.—Why is he helpless to paint?
B. —Because there is nothing to paint and nothing to paint with.

The Unnamable in just this way has nothing to write and nothing to write with ('I can't go on,' he ends, 'I'll go on.'). He is one step beyond even Malone, who has an exercise book and the stub of a pencil, and the will to write a story. ('I did not want to write,' Malone writes, 'but I had to resign myself to it in the end. It is in order to know where I have got to, where he has got to.' [Who is 'he'? His character Macmann? Or Beckett?] 'At first I did not write, I just said the thing. Then I forgot what I had said.') So Malone forces out of himself sentences like, 'He attended classes with his mind elsewhere. He liked sums but not the way they were taught,' and soon dismisses the paragraph ('What tedium'). Other paragraphs go unwritten: 'In his country the problem—no, I can't do it.'

'How false all this is,' Malone also remarks of what he writes about himself. 'No time now to explain. I began again. But little by little with a different aim, no longer in order to succeed but in order to fail.'

In order to fail: in order to accept the inexpressible, which will seep through any membrane art's alchemy can contrive. Severe words have been spoken about 'imitative form', an aesthetic fallacy which mimics the inexpressible by the unintelligible. But here we encounter Beckett the syntactician, whose beautiful sentences are never unintelligible, nor ever deficient in neo-classical linkage the one to the next, except when a sudden rage seizes the speaker, or a grimace of wilfulness passes across his face. (Men are prey to such episodes, that is understandable.) So like some Henry Moore sculpture, shaping the empty spaces which perforate it, a Beckett play or novel locates and shapes unreason, some unsubduable stuff which permeates the universe and is not to be abolished by refusal to think about it.

It has long been premised that the old rational linkages Jane Austen cherished account for only a fraction of either human conduct or human fortune. We must therefore admit the irrational to our imaginings. But by tacit agreement we can only do so when we have some way of making it seem rational: for example the formulae of psychoanalysis, which admit the raging id but stamp its passport, or the formulae of surrealism, which subdue the inexplicable to a trivial mathematic by which any instance claims insouciant equality with any other. The mysteriousness around the Beckett cosmos is unsubdued, neither equipped with identity papers nor toyed with as Franklin's kite toyed with the lightning. We defer to its circumambient presence, even while we cherish the rituals round which it seeps: the symmetries of syntax and order, the luminous precisions of phrase.

Each time we confront a new Beckett work we are installed in some new world, a world where men wait, a world where women sink into the sand, a world where couples lie barely breathing in symmetrical entombment. We deduce the world's rules of order, and adduce pertinent memories of other orders. We must actively adduce such memories; the books and plays do not solicit analogy. Though *Lessness* recalls a sestina and *Godot* a succession of music-hall turns, *Lessness* and *Godot* do not protect themselves by hinting that nothing need unsettle, that some familiar paradigm is merely putting forth an instance. They are content to seem as strange as they are. Living with their strangeness, we gradually discover for ourselves how traditional they are. This is in part to guess that traditional procedures may have always served to shape voids, though never explicitly.

Certainly one use of tradition has been to protect novelty. Alexander Pope, having written his *Pastorals* (after Vergil), his *Essay on Criticism* (after Horace) and his *Rape of the Lock* (after rumours of a Greek mock-epic), next wrote a long poem in couplets, full of details that might have been calculated to shock Queen Anne's polite subjects. Heads are struck off, men are disembowelled, a corpse is dishonoured, capricious heaven trifles with men's affairs. Had aesthetic outrage been a penal offence, it might have earned Pope a session in the pillory. Instead it earned him immeasurable esteem, being shielded by a few words on the titlepage which tell us that it transposes into modern words the *Iliad* of Homer, from fidelity to which its savageries derive. We may fancy literary archaeologists in some future deprived by catastrophe of all Homeric lore, struggling to assimilate this queer bloody poem to the rest of their understanding of the Augustans. It is in a not dissimilar way, sometimes through ignorance of precedents, sometimes through failing to adduce them, that we apprehend late in the twentieth century the theatre and fiction of Samuel Beckett.

In understandably dwelling on his novelties, criticism has only begun its work. It has brought forward no traditions with which to align him, and placed him instead with two or three other playwrights in an *ad hoc* category, the Theatre of the Absurd. But he and Genet and Ionesco are alike chiefly in their dissimilarity to Ibsen, and already Ionesco commences to seem trivial. It is not a useful bracketing. Harold Hobson deserves credit for discerning in Hamm a 'toppled Prospero', thus alerting us to surmise that *Endgame* has more in common with *The Tempest* and *Hamlet* than with *Rhinoceros*. This is not (emphatically not) to equate Beckett with Shakespeare, simply to emphasize that his theatre, with its extensive solo parts, prolongs the theatricality of the English Renaissance, though with the difference that his actors cannot really believe in the salvations of rhetoric. Marlowe's *Tamberlaine*:

> Our souls, whose faculties can comprehend
> The wondrous architecture of the world,
> And measure every wandering planet's course,
> Still climbing after knowledge infinite,
> And always moving as the restless spheres,
> Will us to move ourselves and never rest . . .

It would be Hamm's joy, to make a speech like that. His 'Can there be misery . . . loftier than mine?' bespeaks comparable self-regard if not comparable optimism. Alas, 'the wondrous architecture of the world' is incomprehensibly crumbling around him where he sits in his 'shelter'.

It was T. S. Eliot, we may remember, who defined for our time the use of Shakespearean or Marlovian rhetoric: the character who utters those mighty lines, Eliot said, is 'cheering himself up', tonguing and cherishing, often when all else is lost, the incomparable satisfactions of the adequate phrase. Winnie with her 'classics' is doing something very similar, and so is Pozzo when he describes how the sun sets, having taken a seated pose and sprayed his throat with a vaporizer.

Eliot's view of the consolations of rhetoric seemed self-evident by the time Beckett was writing plays, but whimsical if not blasphemous when he advanced it in 1919. (Cheering themselves up? Othello? Antony?) It is hard now to remember for how long Eliot's opinions, like his poems, were ascribed to American perversity, much as Beckett's writings were explained by the hypothesis of constitutional gloom. Both writers have been treacherous models for imitation. Their surface effects are not difficult to simulate, and it has been easy to suppose that their example makes writing easier, since one need not work out schemes of coherence. Beckett has been widely mistaken for an automatic writer who had no use for revision of his first fine spontaneities, and *Prufrock* once looked like the kind of poem a man of any facility could dash off in a morning; did it not disregard the hard inner logic that gives writers so much trouble? Slowly, it became clear that Eliot's poetic enterprise was laborious and constricted, burdened as it was by the moral responsiblity of printing no unnecessary line. Something similar grows clear of Beckett, and the analogy between his present status and Eliot's status a generation ago is compelling.

Eliot's poetic *oeuvre*, it now appears, was—however widely imitated—simply inimitable, so minutely was it constrained by his private purposes, so firmly did it require just that one unique creative intelligence at its centre, always choosing the difficult way, never wooing copiousness, always willing to be silent. In his middle years he called forth an odd kind of critical homage, of which the real theme was the authenticity of the critic's response. Testimony after testimony to *Four Quartets* said nothing new except that one more reader, having read long, felt compelled to testify.

To testify. And similarly, most writing about Beckett is testimonial. Once under his spell, the need to proclaim the experience takes hold, the need to affirm an encounter with something authentic, mysteriously free from the savour of *accomplishment* that is intrinsic to our satisfaction with most writers. Accomplishment is not a word to apply to Beckett. It implies options, this deed rather than that. But to compliment the author of *How It Is* would be like complimenting an honest man for honesty, and so entangling yourself in the gauche implication that he made a choice, chose not to behave shabbily. Beckett's writing conveys no sense of choice. We are apt to feel that each book, each play, is as it is because it must be. Nor in the same way did it ever seem as though Eliot, with a choice of several unwritten poems, chose to write *Burnt Norton*, let alone that any line of *Burnt Norton* could be otherwise than it is.

So rare, so entangled with the religious conscience, is this air of totally committed inevitability that literary criticism has no terminology for it. Since it is in part Post-Symbolist, the kind of distant analogies that free the mind are unavailable. There is no comfortable way to articulate it, not even by the purely literary strategy of pressing a parallel between Beckett and Eliot. Still, let us press it. Prufrock was perhaps Eliot's Belacqua, Sweeney his Murphy; his questor after meaning in a deprived land who becomes many other persons—Tiresias, the Phoenician sailor, the one-eyed seller of currants—recalls those Beckett figures whose names often begin with 'M', who melt into one another and claim to have invented one another, and whose life is a harassed journeying. Both men had academic backgrounds, both meant to teach philosophy, both became expatriated instead. And both are marked by inaccessibility, though Beckett's retirement is behind a closed door and an unlisted phone whereas Eliot's was behind an array of roles. And the speech of both men, what we know of it, is apothegmic and characterized by eloquent silences. And Beckett will no more explain his work than Eliot would. Eliot often claimed not to know, not to remember; someone else, some prior self wrote the poem, so his protest would run, someone annihilated in the very act of writing it, so that the later man of the same name can offer only guesses no better than yours. Beckett says he does not know very much about his people, and when pressed will sometimes consult his own text with the fresh curiosity of a scholarly enquirer, turning in the light pages written down in the dark.

The striking differences need not be enumerated: between the poet-playwright and the novelist-playwright, between the great critic who commanded impressive assent and the man who professes as few opinions as possible and has signed a vanishingly small number of reviews; above all between the formally committed Christian and the Irish deviser of rigorous afterlives for whom the one Paradise is the one we lost long ago when (like Krapp) we did not know we had it. Both had intense non-conformist Christian upbringings, and it would be a nice exercise, probably feasible but probably also barren, to represent Eliot's Anglo-Catholicism as a development finally equivalent to Beckett's troubling of deaf heaven. Certainly what is accessible and germane is an equal devotion, rigorous and ascetic, to the scrupulously written word, which Eliot practised and Beckett practises with an austerity that deflects the charge that a religion is being made out of art.

How trivial—that was a lesson Eliot taught us—the religion of art was finally; how provincial, how unhistorical, how impoverished. His explicit profession of Christianity—something he might have been expected to keep to himself as he did most personal details—was in part a way to make this point. 'Anglo-Catholic, Royalist, Classical', he wrote, to mark off a terrain in which one need not consecrate one's intentness to book-reviewing. In making no profession of any faith, not even in art, Beckett has established that a like quality of devotion to the word not only need not be a writer's substitute religion, but need not encroach on a reader's religious impulses. He believes in the cadence, the comma, the bite of word on reality, whatever else he believes, and his devotion to them, he makes clear, is a sufficient focus for a reader's attention. In the modern history of literature at least he is a unique moral figure, not a dreamer of rose-gardens but a cultivator of what will grow in the waste land, who can make us see the exhilarating design that thorns and yucca share with whatever will grow anywhere.

Notes on the Text

1. An 'Enueg' was a Provençal poem of revulsion. *Echo's Bones* uses two other Provençal categories, the 'Alba' or dawn-song and the 'Serena', a tranquil night-piece. As for the other titles, 'Dortmunder' is a brand of German beer under the spell of which one poem was written; 'Sanies' is Latin for pus; 'Malacoda' is Dante's deceitful demon (*Inferno* xxi. 76), used as a pseudonym for an undertaker; 'Da Tagte Es' (it was dawn) is a phrase of Walther von Vogelweide's. For 'Echo's Bones' see Ovid, *Metamorphoses* iii, 341–401.

2. Lost in the English version, which offers no equivalent for '*rideau*'.

3. In the unpublished *Dream of Fair to Middling Women*, quoted in Harvey, *Samuel Beckett, Poet and Critic*, 340–1.

4. Thus, since *Omne animal post coitum triste est*, the information that shortly after reaching a hilltop with Winnie Belacqua 'began to feel a very sad animal indeed' enables us to deduce what they have been up to.

5. Recalling the last five lines of *Paradise Lost*, we divine that they explored an Eden of sorts. To make us divine an action by completing a quotation is part of Beckett's procedure at this stage. Not later.

6. My thanks to my colleague Professor Donald Guss for the notes on which the note on the chess game is based.

7. 'His retribution slips my mind.'

'Drowned in a puddle,' said Neary, 'for having divulged the incommensurability of side and diagonal.'

'So perish all babblers,' said Wylie.

8. And the text specifies a nightly displacement of almost one minute, though an annual revolution would require slightly less than one degree. Mathematics, even, is somewhat warped in the domain of Knott.

9. I pause to record the impression that while there are some semi-colons in *Murphy* there are none in Beckett's later fiction. But I have no intention of scanning some thousand pages simply to see if this is correct.

10. A fourth, *Premier Amour*, was for some reason withheld from French publication for twenty-five years, and is still not available in English.

11. 'Extraordinary how mathematics help you to know yourself,' remarked Molloy of a different weakness.

12. Alec Reid, *All I Can Manage, More Than I Could*, Dublin 1968, 21–2.

13. There are ironies in the assertion, by Beckett's close friend Ludovic Janvier, that some such revelation, one evening in Ireland in 1945, preceded the 'implosion' of writings that made him famous.

14. Adumbrated by Molloy, who rammed into his mother's 'ruined and frantic understanding' a code of knocks on the skull.

15. Psalm 103, 15–16: 'As for man, his days are as grass: as a flower of the field, so he flourisheth. For the wind passeth over it, and it is gone; and the place thereof shall know it no more.' The Psalm continues, 'But the mercy of the Lord is from everlasting to everlasting upon them that fear Him.' But not here in the mud, where they have lost the ability to think of Him.

16. Vivian Mercier's phrase.

17. For instance the Olin Library, Washington University, St Louis. For ten successive drafts of the thousand-odd words of *Bing* (in English, *Ping*) see Federman and Fletcher, *Samuel Beckett: His Works and His Critics*, Appendix II, 325–343.

18. In *Seven Types of Ambiguity*, 1930, Chapter I.

19. I did not work this out for myself. It derives from a key, ascribable to the author, which I have through the kindness of Mr John Calder.

Biographical Note

Samuel Beckett, playwright, poet, novelist and 1969 Nobel Laureate in literature, was born in the Dublin suburb of Foxrock on Good Friday the 13th, 1906, to prosperous Irish-Protestant parents. He attended Portora Royal School and Trinity College, Dublin, where he took his degree in the spring of 1928. In Paris, an exchange student at the Ecole Normale Supérieure, he published (1930) an ironically avant-garde poem, *Whoroscope*, and composed a monograph on Proust. He then returned to Ireland and commenced teaching at Trinity, but late in 1931 suddenly jettisoned the academic life and commenced a vagabond period (Dublin, London, Germany) during which he composed the stories in *More Pricks Than Kicks* (1933), the poems of *Echo's Bones* (1936), and the novel *Murphy* (published 1938). In 1936 he settled in Paris, which has been his home ever since.

When the war broke out he was in Ireland, but with a certain stubborn perversity made his way back to Paris just in time to be caught in the Occupation. Resistance activities endangered him, and he fled to the Unoccupied Zone, where he laboured in potato fields and wrote *Watt* (published 1953) in the evenings. Back in Paris after the war, and now writing exclusively in French, he entered on an amazing creative period of which *En Attendant Godot* and the three novels *Molloy, Malone Meurt, L'Innommable* are the best-known issue. By the mid-1950s *Waiting for Godot* was being performed, discussed, alluded to and read in England, America, and most of Europe. English versions of the French novels followed, and the major new plays *Endgame* (1958), *Krapp's Last Tape* (1958) and *Happy Days* (1961). *Comment c'est* (1961), ambiguously a novel, became *How It Is* in 1963. Commissions from the BBC led to radio plays (*All That Fall, Embers, Words and Music*) and a work for television (*Eh Joe*). In 1964 Buster Keaton starred in Beckett's one film script, a short work called *Film*.

Beckett writes everything twice, in French and in English, to similar standards of scrupulous excellence. Recently he has specialized in very short enigmatic texts, implying vast visionary works of which they resemble broken pieces. He lives in Paris with his wife Suzanne, but is not to be found in the telephone book nor the street directory.

Bibliography

Beckett writes everything twice, in English and in French. Conventional title-page formulas—'Translated from the French by the author', or '*Traduit de l'anglais par l'auteur*'—should be understood to designate a second traversing, phrase by phrase, of ground already mapped, performed with an intensity of concentration appropriate to new composition. This is true even when a collaborator's name appears.

The French-language versions are published by Editions de Minuit, Paris. In America, the English-language versions are published by Grove Press, New York. United Kingdom readers must consult the lists of two publishers: Faber and Faber for the dramatic works, Calder and Boyars for the rest. It seems pointless to use space here for largely repetitive lists of titles.

The various printings, editions and critiques up to 1968 are exhaustively surveyed in Raymond Federman and John Fletcher, *Samuel Beckett: His Works and His Critics, an Essay in Bibliography* (Berkeley, Los Angeles and London, University of California Press, 1970).

The first book devoted entirely to Beckett appears to have been Niklaus Gessner's *Die Unzulänglichkeit der Sprache* (Zurich, 1957). Since then an extensive critical literature has appeared in English, French and German, not to mention at least one distinguished work in Italian (Aldo Tagliaferri's *Beckett e l'iperdeterminazione letteraria*: Milan, 1967). I append a selected alphabetical listing of English-language books. For articles, reviews, and dissertations the reader should consult Federman and Fletcher's Bibliography.

Abbot, H. Porter, *The Fiction of Samuel Beckett: Form and Effect* (Berkeley and Los Angeles 1973).

Abel, Lionel, *Metatheater: A New View of Dramatic Form* (New York 1963).

Barnard, G.C., *Samuel Beckett: A New Approach* (New York 1970).

Calder, John, ed., *Beckett at Sixty, a Festschrift* (London 1967).

Coe, Richard N., *Beckett* (Edinburgh and London 1964; New York 1964, retitled *Samuel Beckett*).

Cohn, Ruby, *Samuel Beckett: The Comic Gamut* (New Brunswick, N.J. 1962).

Doherty, Francis M., *Samuel Beckett* (London 1971).

Esslin, Martin, ed., *Samuel Beckett: A Collection of Critical Essays* (Englewood Cliffs, N.J. 1965).

Esslin, Martin, *The Theatre of the Absurd* (New York 1961; London 1962).

Federman, Raymond, *Journey to Chaos: Samuel Beckett's Early Fiction* (Berkeley and Los Angeles 1965; London 1966).

Fletcher, John, *The Novels of Samuel Beckett* (London 1964).

Fletcher, John, *Samuel Beckett's Art* (London 1967).

Friedman, Melvin J., ed., *Samuel Beckett Now: Critical Approaches to his Novels, Poetry and Plays* (Chicago 1970).

Harvey, Lawrence E., *Samuel Beckett: Poet and Critic* (Princeton 1970).

Hassan, Ihab, *The Literature of Silence: Henry Miller and Samuel Beckett* (New York 1968).

Hayman, Ronald, *Samuel Beckett* (London 1968).

Hesla, David H., *The Shape of Chaos: an Interpretation of the Art of Samuel Beckett* (Minneapolis 1971).

Hoffman, Frederick J., *Samuel Beckett: The Language of Self* (Carbondale, Ill. 1962).

Kenner, Hugh, *Samuel Beckett: A Critical Study* (New York 1961; London 1962; augmented edition, Berkeley and Los Angeles 1968).

Kenner, Hugh, *Flaubert, Joyce and Beckett: The Stoic Comedians* (Boston 1962; London 1964).

Mercier, Vivian, *The Irish Comic Tradition* (London 1962).

Reid, Alec, *All I Can Manage, More Than I Could: An Approach to the Plays of Samuel Beckett* (Dublin 1968).

Robinson, Michael, *The Long Sonata of the Dead: A Study of Samuel Beckett* (London 1969; New York 1969).

Scott, Nathan A., *Samuel Beckett* (London 1965).

Simpson, Alan, *Beckett and Behan, and a Theatre in Dublin* (London 1962).

Index of Works and Characters

General Index